The Yellowstone Park Foundation's
Official Guide to
Yellowstone National Park

©R Puppetti/age fotostock

OFFICIAL GUIDE **YELLOWSTONE NATIONAL PARK**

Special thanks to **Canon U.S.A., Inc.** and **Michelin North America, Inc.** for assistance in the creation of this guide, and to the **Yellowstone National Park Division of Interpretation** for factual information and review.

Yellowstone Park Foundation

President	Karen Bates Kress
Corporate Relations Manager	Thomas R. Porter
Director of Communications	Christine Weinheimer

Xanterra Parks & Resorts

Director of Sales and Marketing	Rick Hoeninghausen

Michelin Travel and Lifestyle North America

General Manager	Cynthia Clayton Ochterbeck
Project Manager	Robert Rattray
Editor	Gwen Cannon
Contributing Writers	Valerie Pascoe, Steven Olsen
Production Manager	Natasha G. George
Cartography	Andrew Thompson
Photo Editor	Yoshimi Kanazawa
Photo Researcher	Nicole D. Jordan
Proofreader	Wayne H. Heath
Design	Chris Bell
Layout	Nicole D. Jordan
Cover Layout	Michelin Travel and Lifestyle North America

Contact Us	**Michelin Travel and Lifestyle North America** One Parkway South Greenville, SC 29615, USA travel.lifestyle@us.michelin.com www.michelintravel.com
Special Sales	For information regarding bulk sales, customized editions and premium sales, please contact us at travel.lifestyle@us.michelin.com www.michelintravel.com

WELCOME TO YELLOWSTONE NATIONAL PARK

Every trip you make to Yellowstone should be as magical as your first. Every visitor benefits from knowing more about the park and the many places where that magic can be found. We have created this guide as a comprehensive overview of the park's numerous facets and facilities to enhance your experience and appreciation of the marvel that is Yellowstone.

Home to the largest concentration of wildlife in the lower 48 states, Yellowstone is an important habitat for several endangered, threatened, and declining species. It also holds more geysers, hot springs and other hydrothermal features than the rest of the world combined. Its rich history is intertwined with the history of the American West. Behind the scenes, there is an organization working to ensure that these natural and cultural treasures endure for all time.

The **Yellowstone Park Foundation** is the official fund-raising partner of Yellowstone National Park, created to fund special projects and programs that protect, preserve, and enhance Yellowstone. Since its inception in 1996, the Yellowstone Park Foundation has raised more than $65 million and funded more than 200 important projects and initiatives in the park, providing a "margin of excellence." Past accomplishments include:

- raising $15 million to help fund the state-of-the-art **Old Faithful Visitor Education Center,** which opened in August 2010 [see p38];

- supporting the **Yellowstone Wolf Project**, since 1996, providing funds for critical monitoring and research on wolves' impact on the ecosystem;

- restoring the historic landscape at **Artist Point**, the famous promontory overlooking the Grand Canyon of the Yellowstone River;

- funding research to support native **cutthroat trout restoration** and conservation in Yellowstone;

- rehabilitating more than 100 miles of trails, to date, through the $2-million **Trails Fund Initiative**;

- providing financial support to preserve the park's **several-million-piece museum collection** of rare art, documents, photographs, and specimens;

- **funding the excavation and preservation of artifacts** from eroding, prehistoric archaeological sites.

Important work like the above cannot be accomplished without the generous support of Friends of Yellowstone. Learn more about how you can participate directly in the stewardship of Yellowstone at **www.ypf.org**.

We hope that this guide enriches your visit to this magnificent place.

HOW TO USE THIS GUIDE

INTRODUCTION

The initial chapter opens with an overview of **The Park Today.** The park's geology and topography as well as its varied flora and fauna are described in the **Nature** section. The **History** section spans the park's origins up to current times. **The Park's Future** touches on "green" and other initiatives and plans for the park.

PRACTICAL INFORMATION

The blue-bannered PRACTICAL INFORMATION chapter provides important information to help you **organize your visit** such as useful websites, park entrances and road closures, and how to get there and get around. **Itineraries** for 1, 2 and 5 days are outlined. A section on **basic information** closes the chapter.

EXPLORING YELLOWSTONE

This chapter explores the varied **sights** to see in the park and the many **activities** that invite your participation. The park's Principal Sights are presented by region (seven of them), each featuring the most interesting area sights, **hikes**, park **programs** and other activities, as well as a detailed **Driving Tour**.

ADDRESSES

In this final chapter, the park's **lodges** and inns, cabins and campsites, cafes, restaurants, **bookstores** and other places to shop are organized by category. Amenities and reservations process are described.

Sidebars

Throughout the guide you will find colored text boxes with lively anecdotes, detailed history and background information.

☺ Insider Tips ☺

Advice boxes found in this guide contain practical tips and valuable information authored by experts who know the park well.

STAR RATINGS★★★

Michelin has given star ratings for more than 100 years. If you're pressed for time, we recommend you visit the ★★★ or ★★ sights first:

★★★ Highly recommended
★★   Recommended
★   Interesting

MAPS

☺ A map of the **color-coded** seven regions of the park can be found on the inside front cover, for quick reference.

☺ A map of the park's Principal Sights, many bearing the **Michelin stars**, can be found on the inside back cover, for an **at-a-glance view** of what there is to see and the roads that will take you there.

All maps in this guide are oriented north, unless otherwise indicated by a directional arrow.

RECOGNITION PAGES

At the back of the guide are several pages that acknowledge the corporations and organizations who support the work of the Yellowstone Park Foundation. Without their commitment, this guide would not be possible.

CONTENTS

©Gwen Cannon/Michelin

NPS Photo by Jim Peaco

©Gwen Cannon/Michelin

INTRODUCTION

The magic of a visit to Yellowstone National Park extends beyond the remarkable scenery, astonishing geology and captivating wildlife. It's a vacation experience that provides millions of visitors with the opportunity to connect with nature, the past and ourselves at one of the most significant and awe-inspiring wonderlands in the world.

THE PARK TODAY

Perched on a high plateau bisected by the Continental Divide in the northern Rockies of Wyoming and parts of Montana and Idaho, Yellowstone remains America's oldest and grandest national park.

Spanning a multifaceted terrain of 3,472sq mi—more than Rhode Island and Delaware combined—Yellowstone is perhaps best known for its geological wonders like **Old Faithful Geyser, Mammoth Hot Springs,** and **Grand Canyon of the Yellowstone**. It is one of the last remaining strongholds of the grizzly bear, and has, in recent years, gained additional attention with the reintroduction of wolves.

The park is highly **accessible by car**. Its 466 miles of roadways can be reached from five different entrances. And while there is limited public transportation operating inside the park, one authorized concessioner and several area tour companies provide guided motorized transport. Configured like the number 8, two paved roads, known as the **Grand Loop**, compose the primary routes in the park. These routes provide the most readily accessible view of iconic park sites, yet the majority of Yellowstone's 3 million annual visitors glimpse a mere 3 percent of the entire park. Exploring more remote areas can be accomplished with careful planning and by hiking or guided horse trip.

During the **summer months**, visitors are assisted by the Park Service's 800 **peak-season employees**. Among these staffers are experts in geology,

Below: *Sunrise, Yellowstone Lake*

YPF Photo by Tom Porter

Yellowstone is one of the finest wild lands left on the earth. It remains a secure home and nursery for nearly all the species of animals and plants that resided here hundreds of years ago. Yellowstone has more variety than any of the other national parks: extensive wildlife populations, Yellowstone Lake—a large high altitude clean lake—hundreds of waterfalls, extensive remote mountain ranges, streams that contribute to the headwaters of some of the major rivers of the American West—the Missouri and the Columbia —one of the largest known volcanic calderas on earth, as well as more than half of all the geysers in the world, and this is only part of a long list.

Tom Murphy
Author and natural history photographer

botany, wildlife, history, education and recreation. The park is also utilized by hundreds of researchers, many of them making scientific breakthroughs by studying unique organisms found only in Yellowstone.

NATURE

Some 2.1 million years ago, the earth exploded in the first of three grand blasts, darkening skies across the planet's surface with ash. The 1,500sq mile **Yellowstone Caldera** was created by the most recent blast, just 640,000 years ago, which utterly dwarfs the eruption of Mount St. Helens in 1980. Yellowstone boasts some 10,000 **hydrothermal features**—more than anywhere else on the planet—as the result of a hot spot in the earth's crust that originated near the southern border of Oregon and Idaho, 300 miles to the southwest, about 17 million years ago. The lava flows of the Snake River Plain trace the "movement" of this hot spot as the continental plate slides southwesterly above the source of heat, a **magma plume** rising from deep within the earth. The plume melts the earth's crust and transfers its heat, resulting in hydrothermal features here that are far more numerous than at any other site in the world.

Hydrothermal Features

Geysers – Yellowstone's 300-plus geysers represent the largest concentration in the world. The most famous, **Old Faithful Geyser**, is joined by hundreds of others varying in size and regularity. Their off-and-on behavior is controlled partly by constrictions in their subsurface plumbing. Two categories are found in the park: **fountain geysers**, which erupt from broad pools, and **cone geysers,** which burst through narrow, cone-shaped rock vents. Originating from the same source underground, these geysers erupt into the sky in myriad ways. **Riverside Geyser**, in Upper Geyser Basin, shoots at an angle across the Firehole River, often forming a rainbow in its mist. **Castle Geyser** erupts from a cone-shaped medieval ruin. **Grand Geyser** explodes in a series of powerful bursts that tower above the surrounding area.

INTRODUCTION

Echinus Geyser spouts up and out to all sides, like fireworks do. And **Steamboat Geyser**, the largest in the world, reaching heights of 300ft to 400ft.

Hot Springs – Sparkling jewels among the park's hydrothermal features, Yellowstone's hot springs have colorful names like **Morning Glory, Emerald** and **Sapphire**. Compared with geysers, their plumbing is less constricted, and water flows continuously to the surface. Some springs form small hot rivers, while others create deep-blue or green pools.

Fumaroles – Fumaroles, or **steam vents**, are the hottest of hydrothermal features. They result from boiling beneath the ground, as opposed to on the surface. At sites like **Roaring**

Mountain, the result is a hillside of hissing steam and spewed gases.

Mudpots – Turbulent mudpots are highly **acidic features** that plop and gurgle, making them some of the park's most memorable sights. Microorganisms help convert hydrogen sulfide to sulfuric acid, which breaks down rock into clay. Various gases escape through the wet clay mud, causing it to bubble and ooze and emit a rotten-egg stench. The consistency of the mud varies from thick to soupy at features like **Artist Paint Pot** and **Fountain Paint Pots**.

Geologic Features

Canyons – Yellowstone's hydrothermal activity is also partially responsible for the formation of the **Grand Canyon of the Yellowstone**, carved over thousands of years by the erosive waters of the Yellowstone River. The brilliant gold color of its rhyolite rock is due to iron compounds "cooked" by hydrothermal activity.

Mountain Ranges – The park includes four mountain ranges, two of which, the **Washburn Range** and the **Red Mountains**, are completely enclosed within park boundaries. The other two stretch across multiple states and extend far beyond the borders of the park. The **Gallatin Range** begins about 75 miles north of Yellowstone

Geyser

Hot Spring

Fumarole

Mudpot

Porous Rock Layer

Porous Rock Layer

©Henri Choimet/Michelin

Based on Robert Hynes' illustration for the National Park Service.

near Bozeman, Montana, and covers the northwest corner of the park. The largest range in the park, the **Absaroka**, starts approximately 80 miles north of the park near Livingston, Montana, along the Yellowstone River, and runs southward through the entire eastern side of Yellowstone.

Plants

Yellowstone is home to more than 1,150 species of vascular plants, of which about 218 are non-native. Protecting the area from exotic plant invasion has become a focus of park management. Three endemic species of plants call Yellowstone home: **Ross's bentgrass, Yellowstone sand verbena** and Yellowstone **sulfur buckwheat**. Wildflowers such as **lupine** and **arnica** often grow under the forest canopy, while spring beauties, glacier lilies and steer's head display color in open meadows, announcing spring in the park.

Lodgepole Pine – This tree covers 60 percent of the park and comprises 80 percent of its forested areas. Common in recently burned areas, many of the female trees spread their seeds only after exposure to fire.

Fireweed – Prolific after the 1988 park fires, this plant features radial, symmetric magenta or pink blossoms. Often abundant in wet calcareous to slightly acidic soils in open fields, pastures, and especially burned-over lands, fireweed gets its name from its tendency to quickly colonize open areas with little competition.

Ross's Bentgrass – This species, which rarely grows taller than 6 inches, is found only in the geyser basins along the Firehole River and at Shoshone Lake. The temperature within an inch of the surface under this grass normally hovers at 100°F.

Yellowstone Sand Verbena – This endemic plant, with its white flowers and sticky foliage, can be seen along the shore of Yellowstone Lake growing close to the sand surface.

Yellowstone Sulfur Buckwheat – Several types of sulfur buckwheat grow in the park, but this variety, with its densely hairy upper surface and yellow flowers, grows along the edges of thermally influenced sites from Madison Junction to Upper Geyser Basin.

Wildlife

Yellowstone's residents include grizzly bears, wolves, elk, bison, pronghorn, moose and 322 species of birds. At the dawn of each spring, nature puts on a vivid display as the environment comes back to life after the long winter. The air is filled with bird song along with a chorus of amphibians and insects. Elk, bison, and deer birth and raise calves in the valleys, while large predators hunt to feed their young.

INTRODUCTION

The winter months also provide a dramatic backdrop for wildlife viewing.

Amphibians

• **Blotched Tiger Salamander** – The only salamander in Yellowstone, it can be seen in the Lamar Valley late April to June. Light olive or brownish black in color, adults are about 9 inches in size.

• **Boreal Chorus Frog** – In late afternoon and early evening from April to early July, this frog makes a sound like a thumb running over a comb's teeth.

• **Boreal Toad** – Exhibiting a stocky body and blunt nose, Yellowstone's only toad can grow up to four inches long.

Birds

Yellowstone is surprisingly rich in bird life given the harsh environmental conditions of the landscape. Some 322 species have been documented in Yellowstone, about half of them regular breeders in the park. Several species of raptors stop over in Yellowstone each fall during their annual migration southward. Several species formerly on the endangered list, including the osprey, bald eagle and peregrine falcon, have made a comeback in recent years due to conservation efforts.

Rare Birds of Yellowstone

• **Bald Eagle** – Previously classified as an endangered species, bald eagles can be found near waterways such as Yellowstone Lake and Madison River in summer. In winter, bald eagles can be seen along the **Madison and Gardner Rivers** and in the **Hayden Valley**.
Adult bald eagles are relatively easy to identify due to their large, chocolate brown-colored bodies with a pure white head and tail, and distinctive yellow beak. They typically take five years to acquire adult plumage.

• **Common Loon** – About the size of a large duck or a small goose, the common loon can be found on **Yellowstone Lake**. The common loon population in the park continues to fluctuate from year to year due to variable water levels and shorelines as a result of changing weather conditions. Drought plays a role at some sites.

• **Osprey** – This large, dark-winged, white-bellied bird, which can grow up to two feet long, sports a broad black stripe down the side of its head. Though the osprey population has shown signs of dissipation around Yellowstone Lake due to the decline of cutthroat trout, a major food source, ospreys are doing well parkwide. The best place to view this grand raptor is near lakes and rivers, particularly around the **Grand Canyon of the Yellowstone**.

• **Peregrine Falcon** – The peregrine falcon is one of the world's fastest birds, flying up to 55mph and diving nearly four times faster when striking prey in the air. They can be found in the park from spring until mid-fall when their preferred food sources such as songbirds and waterfowl are nearby.

• **Trumpeter Swan** – This swan, named for its trumpet-like call, is one of the most striking and at-risk birds in Yellowstone. The largest of all North American waterfowl, this elegant bird can reach 4ft in height and measure up to 6ft long from bill to feet. It can be found along the Madison River, in small ponds along the Northeast Entrance Road, and in Hayden Valley.

Mammals

One of the key attractions of the park, 67 mammals live in Yellowstone.

• **Bighorn Sheep** – Bighorn sheep are named for the large, curved horns of the males. Females also have horns, but they are short and only slightly curved. These sheep range in color from light brown to gray or dark, chocolate brown, with a white rear. Rocky Mountain bighorn females weigh up to 200lbs, and males occasionally exceed 300lbs. During the mating season, rams loudly butt heads while battling for females. The crack of horns can sometimes be heard up to a mile away.

• **Bison** – Sometimes called buffalo, the bison is the largest land mammal in North America. In a typical year, more than 3,000 bison roam **the grasslands** of Yellowstone.

Bulls are larger in appearance than cows, and sport thicker beards. For their size, bison are agile and quick, capable of speeds greater than 30mph. In many years, more park visitors are injured by bison than by bears.

• **Black Bears** – Black bears are widely present in Yellowstone, particularly in the **Lamar** and **Hayden Valleys** near Mammoth. They have short, curved claws that are well suited to climbing trees. Behaviorally, black bears are generally less aggressive than grizzly bears and rely on their ability to scale trees to escape predators. Males can weigh more than 300lbs. Despite their name, the color of black bears varies from blond to cinnamon or pure black to brown.

• **Coyotes** – Yellowstone's coyotes are among the largest in the US. Adults range in size from 30lbs to 40lbs. Coyotes differ in appearance from their larger cousin, the gray wolf. Standing

Below: *Pronghorn*

NPS Photo

Beware of Bears

When faced with a threat, black bears are likely to retreat up a tree or flee, rather than act aggressively. However, any bear, particularly a female with cubs, may attack when surprised at close range. Black bears stalk and kill humans, although rarely. Always give black bears and grizzly bears wide berth.

less than 2ft tall, coyotes vary in color from gray to tan, with sometimes a hint of reddish fur. The coyote is a common predator throughout the park, often seen alone or in packs, traveling through open valleys in search of small mammals. They are also skillful hunters of large animals, particularly when they hunt in groups.

• **Elk** – The elk is Yellowstone's most abundant large mammal. The elk population reaches 10,000–20,000 in summer when a large portion of the park provides summer range. The elk population decreases to less than 5,000 in the winter. Males can weigh more than 700lbs, including their tremendous 30lbs antlers. Autumn is a spectacular season to watch elk and listen to them bugle, but elk are aggressive, fast and dangerous at any time of year. Watch them from a safe, legal distance of at least 25 yards.

• **Grizzly Bear** – With a pronounced hump behind its neck, a dish-shaped face and hindquarters that slope downward, a grizzly bear can grow to twice the size of black bears. The park estimates the presence of about 150 grizzlies in Yellowstone, with the best viewing of them in the **Lamar** and **Hayden Valleys** in early morning and evening. Voracious eaters, and more aggressive than black bears, grizzlies feast on fish, game, insects, nuts and plants. Their color ranges from blonde to dark brown.

• **Moose** – The largest member of the deer family, moose can grow up to 7ft at the shoulder. Identified by their large palmate

Left to right: *Elk calf, Bison*

NPS Photo

YPF Photo by Tom Porter

antlers, males can weigh up to 1,300lbs, and females up to 800lbs. Yellowstone's moose population has been in decline since the 1988 fires, which caused a loss of winter habitat. Moose can be unexpectedly aggressive. Keep your distance.

• **Wolves** – Wolves are more readily visible in Yellowstone than anywhere else in the world. The gray wolf was reintroduced to Yellowstone in 1995 after a 7-decade absence. With coats that range in color from snow white to charcoal black, gray wolves can weigh up to 130lbs. As of January 2011, 120 wolves were found in the park. The park's wolf population has become one of Yellowstone's greatest success stories. Prime viewing is in the **Lamar Valley** at dawn or at twilight. Hearing their howl can be a highlight of a park visit.

HISTORY

Yellowstone was a much less hospitable place at the end of the last Ice Age some 10,000 years ago. After thousands of years trapped under thick glaciers, Yellowstone was bubbling back to life, its geological features beginning to spew heat, steam and gas through gradually thinning ice sheets. Richness in food was a key attraction for the early peoples who migrated from Asia roughly 15,000 years ago via the Bering Strait as the ice sheets blanketing North America gradually receded. Yellowstone's extraordinary landscape and otherworldly hydrothermal features also served as a destination for spiritual and ceremonial pilgrimages of early inhabitants.

Human History

The climate for much of the year at this early time was brutal, with numbingly cold temperatures and massive amounts of snow. Discoveries made by archaeologists indicate that the earliest visitors to Yellowstone used **obsidian**— a naturally occurring volcanic rock used today in surgical blades—to hunt animals such as camels, mastodons, elk, bison, black bears and bighorn sheep. When temperatures warmed about 8,500 years ago, at the close of the last Ice Age, some animals like the cold-loving **woolly mammoth** became extinct, while others adapted to the warmer environment. Early man adapted as well. One pervasive group of hunter-gatherers who left behind considerable archaeological evidence were the **Sheepeaters**, a tribe of Shoshone people who lived in small family groups of 10 to 20 people and traveled by foot, hunting with the help of dogs. Their bows, made from the horns of bighorn sheep and decorated with porcupine quills, were considered among the finest bows anywhere in the Yellowstone country and were a prized item of trade among Plains Indians.

The various groups of indigenous people who came to Yellowstone

INTRODUCTION

to live, hunt, fish, mine minerals and engage in ceremonies were the ancestors of as many as 26 tribes associated with the area, including Blackfeet, Crow, Eastern Shoshone, Salish, Sioux, Nez Perce and Shoshone-Bannock.

It was long after Native Americans first "discovered" Yellowstone that French-Canadian **fur trappers** arrived via the Missouri River and the Yellowstone, Madison and Gallatin Rivers in the late 1770s in search of **beaver pelts**. The tribes they traded with probably shared descriptions of Yellowstone's hydrothermal features, but there is no evidence that these trappers and traders actually witnessed the wonders. The trappers did, however, leave their mark by coining the term Yellowstone, or *Rouche Jaune*, and *Teton* to describe the large breast-like peaks of the majestic mountain range to the west.

Era of Exploration

In 1803 **Lewis and Clark's** Corps of Discovery passed through the northern end of the Yellowstone region to explore the vast expanse of land acquired in the Louisiana Purchase. While Lewis and Clark never saw Yellowstone's features, they heard many reports from Indians of a mystically powerful land to the south. The first white man to actually explore the area was probably **John Colter**, who reportedly left the Lewis and Clark party in 1806 on his way back to St. Louis to spend several months trapping in Yellowstone.

Following Colter's visit and his stories of Yellowstone, which were published in the *Louisiana Gazette* in 1810, a trapper named **Daniel Potts** provided his own detailed account to a Philadelphia newspaper in 1827. But their reports fell on deaf ears in the East, where they were largely considered just tall tales.

Generations and rumors came and went before the 1869 **Cook-Folsom-Peterson Expedition** and the **Washburn-Langford-Doane** party braved the wilds to finally separate fiction from fact. The latter group, funded by the Northern Pacific Railroad, was stunned by the awesome truth, and convinced the US Geological Survey to investigate. In June 1871, Survey director **Ferdinand Hayden** explored Yellowstone with 34 men, including painter **Thomas Moran** and photographer **William Henry Jackson**. The evidence they presented was undeniable. On December 18, 1871, a bill was introduced to the US Congress to withdraw the area from settlement and place it under government protection. The following spring, on March 1, 1872, the **world's first national park** was born when President Ulysses S. Grant signed the law declaring that Yellowstone would forever be preserved: "dedicated and set apart as a public park or pleasuring ground for the benefit and enjoyment of the people." **Tourists** began to visit the park, especially when a rail link from

Livingston, Montana, to Gardiner eased access. The park's early civilian administrators couldn't handle the poaching and vandalism, so the US Army took over in 1886, expanding the construction of roads, including **Grand Loop Road**, which was completed in 1905. Automobiles were officially allowed into Yellowstone in 1915.

Three years later, the park was taken over by the **National Park Service** (created in 1916), which manages Yellowstone today.

Historic Places

Among Yellowstone's notable sights are its **historic buildings**. The park contains some 550 structures eligible for, or listed on, the National Register of Historic Places. Five structures are designated **National Historic Landmarks**.

Fort Yellowstone Historic District – Fort Yellowstone-Mammoth Hot Springs Historic District is located in the northwestern portion of the park on a hot springs formation. The buildings on this plateau represent initial development of administrative and concession facilities in the park. The first buildings of Fort Yellowstone were completed here in late 1891.

Historic Backcountry Cabins – The US Army constructed cabins in the late-19th century to provide facilities for troops patrolling the park for poachers. Typically they were erected 16 miles apart, which equaled one day's travel by

horseback. Four cabins surviving from this period are still used by the Park Service for backcountry patrols and researchers.

Lake Fish Hatchery Historic District – This district's buildings are significant for architecture and their role in the conservation policies of the National Park Service. Constructed between 1930 and 1932, the buildings that still remain follow the Rustic Architecture of the National Park Service and its policy of non-obtrusive design that flourished from the 1920s to early 40s.

Old Faithful Historic District – This developed area adjacent to Old Faithful Geyser includes **Old Faithful Inn**, built during the winter of 1903-04. Designed by **Robert C. Reamer**, who wanted the asymmetry of the building to reflect the chaos of nature, the inn is a rustic log and wood-frame structure with gigantic proportions: it is nearly 700ft long and 7 stories high.

Managing the Ecosystem

Throughout park history, and particularly given the sharp increase in the number of visitors over the past several decades, successful management of Yellowstone's delicate ecosystem in tandem with human infrastructure has presented a multitude of challenges.

In the 1920s, a monumental effort to exterminate wolves in Yellowstone rid the park of what was widely perceived as a "destructive threat." In 1995, **wolves from Canada** were reintroduced to the park's Lamar Valley (*see sidebar p59*). The wolves have remained highly visible to visitors, particularly during winter, helping boost tourism in the off-season.

Forest fires have also been a critical part of the life cycle of Yellowstone for at least 12,000 years. During the summer of 1988, which was among the driest in park history, Yellowstone became the site of one of the largest fire-fighting efforts undertaken in the US. Nearly 800,000 acres (or about 35 percent of the park) was affected by these massive lightning-induced fires. During the peak of the conflagration, more than 25,000 firefighters, including units from the Army and the Marines, descended upon Yellowstone to battle the blazes. In September, rain and snow finally brought an end to the fight to suppress the fires. While seen at the time as a calamity, the fires ultimately demonstrated the role of fires in maintaining a **natural balance** in the park. Visitors to Yellowstone in the years following the fires were amazed by the bright displays of **wildflowers** and new life cropping up in unexpected places as the park underwent an extraordinary recovery.

THE PARK'S FUTURE

As record numbers of visitors continue to flock to Yellowstone, the park is increasingly in danger of being damaged. In 1872, legislation that created the world's first national park carried a double mandate: to preserve and protect the land and provide for the enjoyment of people. During a notable portion of the 20th century, the scale tipped in favor of recreation at the expense of preservation. Until the 1960s, Yellowstone was often treated as a drive-through zoo. Bears could be found at park roadsides waiting for food to be handed to them by tourists. Trash was stored in open spaces, non-native fish were introduced into lakes and rivers for sport, and wolves were exterminated.

Fortunately, the pendulum has swung back in favor of nature. Strict guidelines are enforced with respect to human proximity to and interaction with wildlife, hunting is not permitted, fishing is regulated, delicate natural areas are off-limits, and winter air quality has improved. While gradual steps have been taken over several decades to return Yellowstone to its natural state despite substantial human traffic, only recently has a set of formal programs been put into

Photography in Yellowstone has been an important aspect of the history of this place since W.H. Jackson made photographs while on the 1871 Hayden Expedition. His photographs were used to help promote conserving Yellowstone as the first national park in the world.

Tom Murphy
Author and natural history photographer

place to achieve ambitious goals for managing Yellowstone's vast operation more sustainably and responsibly into the future.

Greening the Greenest Place on Earth

Accommodating Yellowstone's annual visitor load of approximately 3 million people while protecting wildlife and carefully preserving the ecosystem is a delicate balancing act. The environmental impact of crowds driving, hiking, eating and sleeping their way through the park is enormous. Yellowstone's 4,000 total employees (including concessioners), 2,000 hotel rooms and 2,000 campsites alone require considerable amounts of fuel, food and electricity, while generating thousands of tons of trash.

Yellowstone National Park administrators, along with concessioner partners, strive to make Yellowstone a leader in environmental sustainability. For its vehicle fleet, the park was an early adopter of **alternative fuels**, and at some park facilities, uses **solar panels** to generate power. In recent years, it has implemented a large-scale **composting program** as well as first-ever pilot projects to recycle propane canisters and bear spray canisters. Xanterra Parks & Resorts, which operates Yellowstone National Park Lodges, created an innovative system to convert their used cooking oil to fuel. This fuel now powers hotel boilers at Mammoth and Old Faithful, a process that is reducing the park's carbon footprint.

In 2009, the Yellowstone Park Foundation launched the **Yellowstone Environmental Stewardship** (YES!) initiative, now part of the broader Greenest Park initiative. It is a public-private partnership that complements existing federally funded projects aimed at decreasing human impact on the park. By 2016, the YES! initiative aims to significantly reduce the park's greenhouse gas emissions and decrease consumption of electricity, fossil fuel and water.

What You Can Do

Donate $1 or more per night of your hotel stay to your final bill to fund research, conservation and education through the Yellowstone Park Foundation. Recycle to help protect the park. Use park recycling bins for aluminum, steel, cardboard, glass, paper, plastic and electronic waste, as well as for propane and bear spray canisters. Bins can also be found in guest rooms at hotels around the park and in campgrounds. Last year alone, more than 40 tons of plastic water bottles were recycled. If every visitor took just these two steps alone, think what the benefit to the park would be.

PARK ITINERARIES

If you are short on time, maximize your visit with these suggested itineraries for from one to five days. If you only have a day to spare, pick the first day option, which hits the highlights. If you're down for the weekend and have a couple of days to explore, use the recommendations up to day two. For longer trips, see the recommendations up to day five. For all park accommodations, *see Overnighting in the Park*.

DAY 1

Morning – Lamar Valley★★ – Arrive early (6am) and enter the park from the Northeast Entrance Road.
Mid-Morning – Grand Canyon of the Yellowstone★★★; Upper Falls★ and **Lower Falls★★** and **Artist Point★★**.
Lunch – Lake Yellowstone Hotel.
Afternoon – Old Faithful★★★; Upper Geyser Basin★★.
Evening – Dinner and overnight at the **Old Faithful Inn★★**.

DAY 2

Morning – Upper Geyser Basin★★; Grand Prismatic Spring★★; Fountain Paint Pots★★.
Lunch – Firehole River Picnic Area.
Early Afternoon – Norris Geyser Basin★★ and the Norris Geyser Basin Museum.
Late Afternoon – Mammoth Hot Springs★★★.

Evening – Dinner at Mammoth Hotel Dining Room. Overnight at Mammoth Hot Springs Hotel.

DAY 3

Morning – Horseback ride (*reserve at Mammoth Hotel*). See the Petrified Tree en route to Tower-Roosevelt Area.
Lunch – Roosevelt Lodge.
Afternoon – Stagecoach ride from Roosevelt Corral.
Evening – Old West Dinner Cookout (reservations required). Overnight at Roosevelt Lodge.

DAY 4

Morning – Day hike to **Tower Falls★★**, then drive through sky-high **Dunraven Pass★**.
Lunch – Canyon Lodge.
Afternoon – Hayden Valley★★ Mud Volcano and Fishing Bridge.
Late-Afternoon – Guided tour of Lake Yellowstone Hotel.
Evening – Lake Butte Sunset Tour. Dinner in Lake Lodge Cafeteria. Overnight at Lake Yellowstone Hotel.

DAY 5

Morning – Natural Bridge Trail.
Lunch – Gull Point Picnic Area.
Afternoon – Scenic cruise on Yellowstone Lake; **West Thumb Geyser Basin★**; Grant Village Visitor Center.
Late Afternoon – Check in at Grant Village lodgings; ask about evening ranger-led interpretive programs.

WHEN TO GO

Yellowstone National Park is one of the most visited national parks in America. The height of visitation is May to October when most interior roads and facilities are open.

Visitation

A total of 3,640,184 people visited the park in 2010. The park experienced record-breaking summer visitation in 2010, exceeding 2.5 million visitors. The 2010-2011 winter season recorded 88,804 visits, a decrease from the previous year most likely due to the heavy snowfall. Winter trips are not uncommon, but they require more planning. Most winter visitors arrive by car, bus or RV at the North Entrance, or by snowcoach or snowmobile at the other three main entrances.

Climate

Most of Yellowstone sits at an **altitude** above 7,500 feet, a location that is a major factor in shaping its climate. Lower elevation areas of the park are generally warmer year-round. As a whole, the park experiences a broad range of weather and **temperatures** (see chart p20). Some snow is the norm in early **spring**, with daytime temperatures hitting the high 40°Fs.

(see chart p20)

INSIDER TIP
PARK WEATHER

🐾 The park's weather is one of the many natural phenomena that makes Yellowstone so unique and spectacular but also very dangerous if you are not prepared. No matter what time of year, be prepared for extreme temperature changes from cold mornings to very hot days. Clothing layers work year-round as they insulate your body from both cold and heat. Summer storms can come up quick in the park, especially thunderstorms with extreme lightning, hail and rain. If you see those ominous black clouds, move inside a building or vehicle. Do not remain on boardwalks or trails. For the safety of you, your family and friends, move indoors as quickly as possible. The time spent inside a building, shelter or vehicle will be time well spent within the safety of those structures.

Suzanne Lewis
Former Yellowstone National Park Superintendent (retired)

Recreational Visitors	2011	2010
June	634,316	694,841
July	906,935	957,785
August	805,173	854,837
Summer Months	2,346,424	2,507,463
(Source: www.nps.gov)		

PRACTICAL INFORMATION

Average Monthly and Annual Temperatures				
Month	Avg. Max. Temp. (°F)	Avg. Min. Temp. (°F)	Avg. Precipitation (Inches)	Avg Total Snow Fall (inches)
Feb	34	13	0.75	10.4
May	60.4	34.3	2	1.5
Aug	78.3	45.3	1.4	0
Nov	38.7	19.2	1	9
Annual	52.8	27.6	15.4	72.1
(Source: www.nps.gov)				

Temperatures gradually rise and may reach the 60°Fs and 70°Fs by late May. Throughout spring, it is important to prepare for nighttime lows below freezing.

By **summer,** temperatures are consistently in the 70°Fs and low 80°Fs. More extreme heat is intermittent. The highest recorded temperature in Yellowstone was 99°F in 2002. Nights tend to cool off and may descend into the 30°Fs or 20°Fs. June is usually a cooler and rainier month; July and August are somewhat drier, with flash thundershowers in the afternoons.

Autumn can be pleasant, even if temperatures average only in the 50°Fs and 60°Fs during the day. Some visitors prefer this milder time of year when there are fewer crowds. Yet it is important to remember that temperatures can drop into the teens at night.

Most of Yellowstone averages 150 inches of **winter** snowfall. Higher elevations have been known to receive between 200 inches and 400 inches of snow. Daytime temperatures hover near freezing; nighttime temperatures often fall well below zero. To check the weather for your trip, go to the National Weather Service's website: www.weather.gov or to www.nps.gov/yell.

What to Bring

Pack clothes for layering. Be ready for snow *and* rain; sudden showers are common in July and August. Most areas of the park see some snow until early June. Conditions can change from warm to cool quickly.

Day packs with reuseable water bottles, snacks, sunscreen, bug repellent, maps and compass are advisable. Bring binoculars and a camera. If you forget something, basic camping gear, personal items and groceries are available in the park.

NPS Photo by Jim Peaco

Backcountry Hiking

If you plan to day hike or take a backcountry trip, preparation is important. Bring bear spray as a precaution. Many backcountry trails necessitate fording streams and small rivers. Proper footgear, convertible pants and waterproof packs are recommended. Bring at least 35ft of rope to suspend packs on a food storage pole. Overnight backcountry camping requires a permit, which is free within 48 hours of your trip. If you request it by mail, a fee will be charged. Trip planners can be downloaded at www.nps.gov/yell.

Fishing

The season runs Memorial Day weekend through the first Sunday in November. For guided trips, see authorized outfitters at www.nps.gov/yell.

KNOW BEFORE YOU GO

Useful Websites

www.nps.gov/yell –National Park Service's official website for Yellowstone National Park.

INSIDER TIP
ANGLERS' GEAR

First time visitors to the park might want to spend a day with a knowledgeable guide as this will save visitors a lot of shoe leather and gasoline. An 8½ or 9ft rod balanced with a 4, 5 or 6 weight line is recommended. A floating weight forward or double-taper line will handle most fly-fishing situations in the park. Full sinking lines can be used for effectively fishing Yellowstone's many lakes. Sink-tip lines are helpful for fishing big nymphs and streamers in the fall season. Felt-soled, chest-high waders are recommended. Lightweight waders with the new breathable fabric are convenient for packing in on backcountry trips. In July and August, anglers can wade some streams with a good pair of wading shoes and wading pants, without waders. Never fish in Yellowstone country without bear spray, rain gear, sun block, sunglasses and insect repellent, and a hat.

Craig Mathews
Nationally recognized fly-fishing guide, Blue Ribbon Flies, West Yellowstone

NPS Photo by Jim Peaco

Left to right: *Aspen trees near Mammoth Hot Springs; Winter, Barronette Peak*

www.ypf.org – Yellowstone Park Foundation's website.

www.greateryellow stonescience.org – Greater Yellowstone Science Learning Center is coordinated by NPS and has statistics on a wide variety of topics.

www.YellowstoneNational ParkLodges.com – Official website for Yellowstone National Park Lodges, operated by Xanterra Parks & Resorts, the authorized lodging concessioner for Yellowstone National Park.

www.yellowstone association.org – Website of the Yellowstone Association, the official educational partner of Yellowstone, which offers field courses and operates bookstores in park visitor centers.

Park Entry

Each private, noncommercial vehicle – $25
Snowmobile or motorcycle – $20
Each visitor entering by foot, bike, skis, etc. (16 years or older) – $12
The above fees are subject to change. They allow entrance to both Yellowstone and Grand Teton National Parks for 7 consecutive days. To re-enter the parks, you must have your admission receipt.

Annual/Lifetime Passes

- **Park Annual Pass** – $80. Provides access for passholder and any passengers in a private non-commercial vehicle at Yellowstone and Grand Teton National Parks for 12 months from date of purchase. Available for purchase at any

of the park's entrances or online at http://store.usgs.gov/pass.
- **Interagency Annual Pass** for passholder and any passengers in a private non-commercial vehicle at most US federal recreation sites.
- **Interagency Senior Pass** for US citizens or permanent residents 62 years and older for lifetime.
- **Access Pass** is free to citizens or permanent residents of the US who have documentation of a permanent medical disability.

Visitor Services

Most **visitor centers** open in April or May and close in September or October. Exceptions are the **Albright Visitor Center** in Mammoth, which is open year round, and the **Old Faithful Visitor Education Center**, which is open mid-April to early November and mid-December to mid-March.
Check the park's website at www.nps.gov/yell or check locally for specific opening and closing dates.

Services and Facilities within the park include:

Boat Rentals and Charters
Campgrounds
Dining
Gas Stations
Horseback Riding
Stores and Gift Shops
Lodging
Medical Facilities
Park Bookstores
Post Offices
Day Care

Lodging and some Campgrounds are run by Xanterra Parks & Resorts. Bookings can be made at www.YellowstoneNational ParkLodges.com or by calling toll free 866-439-7375 (*see Overnighting in the Park*).

Authorized Park Guides/ Outfitters/Service-providers
Businesses, guides and outfitters permitted to operate within Yellowstone include:
Bicycling Shops
Boating Businesses
Fishing Outfitters
Hiking & Backpacking
Nature-related Services
Photo Tours
RV Repair Service
Stock Outfitters

GETTING THERE
By Air
Airports – Yellowstone National Park is served by the following commercial airports year round:
Idaho Falls, ID – Idaho Falls Regional Airport (IDA); 208-612-8221; www.idahofallsidaho.gov/city/city-departments/idaho-falls-regional-airport.html
Bozeman, MT – Bozeman Yellowstone International Airport (BZN); 406-388-8321; www.bozemanairport.com
Cody, WY – Yellowstone Regional (COD); 307-587-5096; www.flyyra.com
Jackson, WY – Jackson Hole Airport (JAC); 307-733-7682; www.jacksonholeairport.com
Yellowstone Airport (WYS) in West Yellowstone, MT, is serviced June to early

September from Salt Lake City, UT. 406-646-7631; www.yellowstoneairport.org.

Airlines
Allegiant Air
(702-505-8888; www.allegiantair.com) – BZN (Las Vegas, Phoenix), IDA (Las Vegas, Los Angeles, Phoenix)
American Airlines
(www.aa.com) – JAC (Seasonal: Dallas/Fort Worth)
Delta (www.delta.com) – BZN (Seasonal: Atlanta, Detroit, Minneapolis/St. Paul); JAC (Seasonal: Minneapolis/St. Paul, Salt Lake City)
Delta Connection
(www.delta.com) – BZN (Minneapolis/St. Paul; Salt Lake City); IDA (Salt Lake City); JAC (Seasonal: Salt Lake City); WYS (Seasonal: Salt Lake City)
Frontier Airlines
(800-872-3608; www.frontierairlines.com) – BZN (Denver); JAC (Seasonal: Denver)
Alaska Airlines/Horizon Air (www.alaskaair.com) – BZN (Seattle/Tacoma)
Seaport Airlines
(888-573-2767; www.seaportair.com) – IDA (Boise)
United Airlines
(www.united.com) – BZN (Seasonal: Chicago-O'Hare, Denver); JAC (Seasonal: Chicago-O'Hare, Denver)
United Express
(www.united.com) – BZN (Chicago-O'Hare, Denver, Seasonal: Los Angeles, San Francisco); COD (Denver); IDA (Denver, San Francisco); JAC (Denver, Seasonal: Los Angeles)

PRACTICAL INFORMATION

By Bus

Greyhound (800-231-2222; www.greyhound.com) has service to Bozeman, Livingston and West Yellowstone, MT. No Greyhound bus goes directly to a Yellowstone entrance, so riders will have to rent a car or take a shuttle to get to Yellowstone. West Yellowstone, MT, located adjacent to the West Entrance, is the closest bus destination to Yellowstone.

By Car

Yellowstone lies primarily in Park County in northwest Wyoming; however, portions of the park extend into Montana and Idaho (*see map inside cover*).
Distances to Yellowstone from major cities:

  Salt Lake City, UT – 375 miles
  Boise, ID – 440 miles
  Denver, CO – 625 miles
  Portland, OR – 825 miles
The park is bordered by Interstate 90 in the north and Interstate 15 to the west.

To approach the park **from the north** from Montana:
I-90 to Livingston, then south on Highway 89 to Gardiner, continuing to the park's North Entrance, or
I-90 to Bozeman, then south via Highway 191 to West Yellowstone, continuing to the park's West Entrance, or
I-90 to Billings, then west to Highway 212 (Beartooth Scenic Highway) south to Silver Gate; from there continue to the park's Northeast Entrance. Subject to closures due to snow, Highway 212 is usually open

Memorial Day to just after Labor Day. Check before you depart.

To approach the park **from the south** from Utah and Idaho:
I-215 north from Salt Lake City to I-15. Drive north on I-15 to Idaho Falls then north on Highway 20; continue to the park's West Entrance, or
just south of Idaho Falls, Highway 26 (from I-15) to Jackson, WY, then north on Highway 89 to the park's South Entrance.

To approach the park **from the east** from Wyoming:
Highway 20 west from Cody to the park's East Entrance, or
State Road 120 from Cody northwest to State Road 296 (Chief Joseph Scenic Highway), then west to Highway 212, continuing to the park's Northeast Entrance.

To approach the park **from the west**:
In Montana, I-90 east, then follow directions from the north (*above*).
In Idaho, I-84 east to I-86 east to I-15 north, then follow directions from the south (*above*).
In Utah, I-80 east or I-15 north to Salt Lake City, then follow directions from the south (*above*).

2012 Road Openings and Closures

Once an entrance opens, it is open 24hrs a day, barring any road construction or bad weather.

These dates are valid for 2012 only. Visit the park's website at www.nps.gov/yell or check locally for exact opening and closing dates beyond 2012. *Note that road openings depend on weather conditions.*

March 1 – East Entrance to Lake Butte over-snow travel ends at 9pm.

March 4 – Mammoth to Norris over-snow travel ends at 9pm.

March 6 – Norris Junction to Madison Junction and Norris Junction to Canyon over-snow travel ends at 9pm.

March 11 – Canyon to Fishing Bridge over-snow travel closes at 9pm.

Mid-March – Non-motorized travel (bicycling, walking, jogging, roller blading, roller skiing, etc.) between West Entrance and Mammoth Hot Springs is initiated, permitted as crews prepare for the summer season.

April 20 – Westside roads open at 8am to motor vehicles. Visitors are permitted to access Norris, Madison, Canyon and Old Faithful through the North and West Entrances.

May 4 – Road connecting Canyon, Fishing Bridge and the East Entrance opens to wheeled vehicles.

May 11 – South Entrance to Grant, West Thumb, Fishing Bridge and Lake over Craig Pass to Old Faithful open for travel to wheeled vehicles.

May 25 – Dunraven Pass (Tower to Canyon) opens to wheeled vehicles.

May 25 – Long Lake Gate over the Beartooth Highway to Red Lodge, Montana, opens to wheeled vehicles.

October 9 – Tower Fall to Canyon Junction and Long Lake via Beartooth Pass to the Montana State line close at 8am.

November 4 – ALL park roads close to the public at 8am except North Entrance to Upper Mammoth Terrace, and Mammoth via Tower Junction to Northeast Entrance.

Mid-December – Most roads open to over-snow travel.

Third Week December – East Entrance Road opens to over-snow travel.

In winter, only two park roads remain open for wheeled-vehicle use: 1) the road between the North Entrance at Gardiner, MT, to the Northeast Entrance at

Park Entrance Openings and Closures		
Gate	Opens	Closes
East	May 6	November 6
West	April 15	November 6
North	Open all year	
Northeast	Open all year (closed Cooke City over Colter Pass to the Chief Joseph Scenic Highway intersection to the Long Lake gate during the winter season until late May)	
South	May 13	November 6

Silver Gate and Cooke City, MT; 2) from Mammoth Hot Springs to the parking area at the Upper Terraces.

GETTING AROUND
Driving in the Park

Yellowstone's main park road, **Grand Loop Road**, forms a figure 8, with roads spurring from it to the five park entrances. This 140-mile stretch of road provides access to Yellowstone's iconic sites. It is narrow and winding, and often steep, so allow plenty of driving time. **Speed limits** are 45mph or less. It is important to watch for pedestrians, bicyclists, motorcyclists and wildlife. When your vehicle is parked, lock it and keep valuables out of sight.

Roads generally open by sections on different dates starting the third Friday in April. Once a section opens, it usually stays open until the first Monday of November. Maintenance, accidents, inclement weather and rock slides may temporarily close a section of a road or cause delays. For **scheduled road improvements**, check at a visitor center or an entrance station.

Storms may cause temporary restrictions in autumn and spring, such as the use of chain or snow tires. All roads are closed to motor vehicle travel in **winter**, except the North Entrance road from Gardiner to Cooke City, MT, which is open all year. In order to leave the park in the winter, drivers must return to the North Entrance.

Car Rental Companies –

A number of car rental companies have offices in the area, especially at regional airports. There are no rental companies within the park.
Avis (www.avis.com)
Budget (www.budget-yellowstone.com)
Enterprise (www.enterprise.com)
Hertz (www.hertz.com)

Bus Tours in the Park

During the summer, park bus tours are operated by **Xanterra Parks & Resorts**. Bus and van tours vary in length, intensity and areas visited. Xanterra also offers "Historic Yellow Bus" tours.

Yellowstone in a Day, otherwise known as the "Grand Loop" tour, is commonly booked by first-time visitors to the park. It runs 10 hours. Buses depart from either Gardiner, MT (near the North Entrance), Mammoth or Old Faithful Inn.

Other bus and van tours include the **Circle of Fire** and **Lamar Valley Wildlife Excursion**.

NPS Photo

Buses leave from Canyon Lodge, Fishing Bridge RV Park, Lake Yellowstone Hotel and Bridge Bay Campground. Xanterra also offers **custom-guided tours** in a variety of vehicles.

Historic Yellow Bus tours are offered in replicas of the original 13-passenger Yellowstone buses. Partial Day Tours include **Wake Up to Wildlife, Picture Perfect Photo Safari, Firehole Basin Adventure** and **Geyser Gazers**. All tours leave from Lake Hotel or Old Faithful Inn except "Wake Up to Wildlife," which departs from Canyon Lodge, Mammoth Hotel or Roosevelt Lodge. Rates do not include tax, utility fee or gratuity. To make reservations, call 307-344-7311 or visit www.Yellow stoneNationalParkLodges.com. Many commercial businesses offer tours originating from towns near Yellowstone. For an exhaustive list, visit www.nps. gov/yell.

The nonprofit **Yellowstone Association** educates park visitors through their bookstores (see page p84) and year-round guided classes offered by their **field institute**. The focus is small-group learning in the field, led by content experts and naturalist guides. Participants can choose multi-day courses such as wolf-watching, photography, or cross country skiing. Private tours are also available. For information and reservations, visit www. yellowstoneassociation.org or call 406-848-2400.

Other Transportation
Bicycles
Bike rentals are located within Yellowstone. **Xanterra Parks & Resorts** rents bicycles at the Old Faithful Snow Lodge. In early spring and late fall, roads are closed to wheeled vehicles. Do not travel at night, stay a safe distance from wildlife and carry bear spray. Bring drinking water and perhaps a first aid kit. For regulations, access www.nps.gov/yell.

Boats
Most of Yellowstone Lake and Lewis Lake are open to motorized boats, but park rivers and streams (except the Lewis/Shoshone Lakes channel) are off limits.
Canoes and non-motorized vessels are allowed on most lakes and rivers. All vessels require a permit. Personal watercraft such as jets skis, airboats and submersibles are prohibited at Yellowstone.

NPS Photo by Jim Peaco

Left to right: Bus tour, Cycling past Castle Geyser

A regulation guide can be found online at www.nps.gov/yell. Outboards and rowboats can be rented from Xanterra Parks & Resorts at **Bridge Bay Marina** on Yellowstone Lake. Xanterra also offers guided boat and fishing trips. Call 1-866-439-7375.

Winter Transport
Snowcoaches/Snowmobiles
Most roads in Yellowstone are open only to snowcoach and snowmobiles mid-December to mid-March. However, two roads do stay open year round: 1) the road between the North Entrance at Gardiner, MT, to the Northeast Entrance at Silver Gate and Cooke City, MT and 2) the road from Mammoth Hot Springs to the parking area at the Upper Terraces.
Check the Park entrances opening and closings chart above for information about the Northeast Entrance.
Visiting the park on a snow-mobile or in a snowcoach is permitted only via a commercial guide. Private snowcoaches and snowmobiles are not allowed in the park. Xanterra Parks & Resorts and a number of other businesses provide winter transportation services. A complete list can be found at www.nps.gov/yell.

ACCESSIBILITY
The free guide *Accessibility in Yellowstone*, available at entrance stations and park visitor centers, describes facilities for wheelchairs and other mobility needs. For more information,

download a pdf of the guide from the park website. The hearing impaired may obtain visitor information through TYY 307-344-2386.

HEALTH AND SAFETY
Altitude
Yellowstone sits mostly above 7,500 feet in altitude. Allow time to acclimate to this high altitude by drinking plenty of water. It is advisable to contact a physician prior to visiting if you have a cardiac or respiratory history. The high altitude brings risk of sun exposure. Long sleeved shirts, hats and sunglasses are recommended. Protect exposed body parts with a high-SPF content sunscreen.

Medical Services
Outpatient medical services are available at Lake, Mammoth and Old Faithful facilities in summer. 24-hour emergency services, ambulances, pharmacy, laboratory and radiology services are available. The Mammoth Clinic operates year-round.

Scalding Water
The waters of hydrothermal features are often above boiling. The surrounding crust can break easily. Stay a safe distance from all hydrothermal areas. Stay on boardwalks and designated trails. Pets are strictly prohibited in hydrothermal areas. Hydrothermal areas are known to emit toxic gases. Leave immediately if you begin to feel sick.

BASIC INFORMATION

Important Numbers

Dial 911 for an emergency.
Yellowstone National Park main number: 307-344-7381; TTY 307-344-2386
Park lodging and Activities: 307-344-7311 or toll-free 866-439-7375; TTY 307-344-5395
Yellowstone Association (books, maps, classes): 307-344-2293
Yellowstone Park Foundation: 406-586-6303 in Bozeman, MT (learn how you can help Yellowstone).

Electricity

Voltage in the US is 120 volts AC, 60 Hz. Foreign-made appliances may need AC adapters (available at specialty travel and electronics stores) and North American flat-blade plugs.

Emergencies

24-hour emergency services are available in the park. Dial 911.

Internet

Xanterra offers wireless Internet through a third party (for a fee) at Old Faithful Snow Lodge and Mammoth Hotel Dining Room Lounge.

Public Toilets

Restrooms are located at visitor centers, scenic areas, picnic areas and all campgrounds. Accessible restrooms are available at all developed areas except West Thumb and Norris.

Smoking

Smoking in the park poses a real fire danger. It is strictly prohibited on all trails and thermal areas. Smoking is allowed in gravel or paved parking areas, in developed campgrounds, adjacent to backcountry fire rings. No smoking is allowed inside any building in Yellowstone. Smokers must be 25ft from a building. **Be extra careful if you smoke**: the largest of the park's 1988 fires started from a discarded cigarette and burned 410,000 acres.

Taxes

A parkwide 4% Wyoming sales tax applies to all purchases. A 2% lodging tax applies in Teton County and a 4% lodging tax applies in Park County.

Telephones/Cells

Cell phone service is generally available at Grant Village, Canyon Village, Mammoth Hot Springs, and Old Faithful. For the most part, cell phone coverage is very limited in the park. Telephones are located in most lodgings' guest rooms, but not in cabins. Telephone booths are available at most facilities and visitor centers.

Water

Due to the high elevation, visitors should drink a lot of water. Facilities and developed areas of the park normally have drinking fountains and spigots to refill water bottles. Potable water is provided at most park campgrounds.

No trip to Yellowstone is complete, especially for first-time visitors, without seeing the Old Faithful Area in the southwest part of the park. In addition to witnessing an ever-reliable eruption of the world's most famous geyser, you'll see a profusion of colorful hot springs, steaming fumaroles and historic structures. Each year, four out of five of the park's three million visitors stop here, making it Yellowstone's most popular attraction. The area offers an abundance of activities in summer and winter, including outdoor and indoor recreation as well as education for groups as well as individuals.

SEE
See map inside front cover.
Old Faithful Geyser★★★
The world's most famous geyser has been spouting with uncanny regularity since it was discovered by the Washburn-Langford-Doane party in 1870. Averaging 135ft in height when it erupts (sometimes reaching 180ft), Old Faithful puts on a show every 65 to 110 minutes. Eruptions last 90 seconds to 5 minutes and spew 3,700 to 8,400 gallons of boiling water. In the July to August peak season, thousands of people wait patiently for an eruption, then scurry to other activities.

Area restaurants fill immediately afterward and clear out just before. The village edging Old Faithful is the park's most developed, with massive parking lots and numerous buildings facing the geyser. The most widely accessible views of the eruptions are from the benches bordering two sides of the geyser, but the open deck off the first balcony in Old Faithful Inn offers seating and an elevated view of the geyser's outbursts. Predicted eruption times are posted in the Old Faithful Visitor Education Center, which provides an excellent indoor viewing space away from the sometimes gusty outdoors.

Left to right: *Old Faithful Inn, Old Faithful Geyser erupting*

NPS Photo by Jim Peaco

©Gwen Cannon/Michelin

Old Faithful Historic District

Situated on the southern end of the Upper Geyser Basin, along Grand Loop Road, this area features several historic buildings. Chief among them is **Old Faithful Inn★★**. Also of significance are Old Faithful Lodge and Lower Hamilton Store, the latter the oldest structure in the district that is still in use. It features a popular "knotty pine" porch with a view of Geyser Hill.

Old Faithful Visitor Education Center

This new center (*see p38*) provides interactive learning opportunities (*see Exhibits below*), as well as postings of Old Faithful's predicted eruption times. It is a highly recommended first stop in your exploration of the park.

Upper Geyser Basin★★

Surrounding Old Faithful is the world's largest concentration of geysers. Better known are **Grand Geyser★**, which unleashes a 200ft fountain every 7-15 hrs; **Riverside Geyser★**, whose stream spurts up to 80ft at 5-6hr intervals; and **Castle Geyser★**, which explodes as high as 90ft twice daily from an ancient 12ft cone.

The basin's hottest pools typically reflect the color of the sky. The best-known spring, **Morning Glory Pool★★**, is not as blue as it once was: its hot-water vent has been clogged by objects thrown into the pool by park visitors, an act that is prohibited.

Midway Geyser Basin★

When Rudyard Kipling visited Yellowstone in 1889, this thermal feature-packed basin was being referred to locally as "Hell's Half Acre." Mist from the wide **Excelsior Geyser** envelops visitors who cross the footbridge and climb past a multicolored bank of the Firehole River.

Grand Prismatic Spring★★

Runoff from this large hot spring, part of the Midway Geyser Basin, has created terraced algae mats, often punctuated by hoof prints from bison. Wooden walkways allow visitors to closely approach the waters. At 370ft across and 120ft deep, rainbow-colored Grand Prismatic is the second-largest hot spring in the world. Other colorful springs nearby include **Turquoise** and **Indigo** springs, known for their striking hues of pale and dark blue.

Lower Geyser Basin

In terms of hot water discharge, no other section of the park compares to this 18sq mile area that averages an estimated 15,300 gallons per minute. The majority of this hydrothermal activity takes place in the Fountain Paint Pots and Firehole Lake (*see Drive below*) areas.

Fountain Paint Pots★★

Visitors are able to view all four types of Yellowstone thermal features (*see illustration p8*) on a short tour of this area. A boardwalk leads past colorful bacterial and algae mats, hot pools and the namesake bubbling "paint pots." Visitors, particularly children, revel in the implied messiness, oozing and rotten-egg stench of the spring's hydrogen sulfide gas. The perpetually active **Clepsydra Geyser★** is especially scenic in winter, when bison wander in front of its plume of steam.

NPS Photo by Jim Peaco

Kepler Cascades

Visible from the Grand Loop Road, this natural delight is easily accessible from a platform a few steps from a parking area. Its three-tiered cascade plunges approximately 150 feet over multiple drops as the Firehole River runs north. Nearby, **Lone Star Geyser** erupts about every 3hrs at heights of up to 40ft (see Hiking below).

DO

Check www.nps.gov/yell and www.YellowstoneNationalPark Lodges.com for current fees and schedules for activities listed.

Summer

Biking — Xanterra Parks & Resorts, the concessioner for the hotels and dining rooms in Yellowstone, rents bicycles at the Old Faithful Snow Lodge. If you plan to bring one, it is subject to the same traffic rules as vehicles. Cycling is permitted on established public roads, parking areas, and designated routes. Bikes are prohibited

INSIDER TIP
GEYSER HILL

One of my favorite places at Yellowstone is the observation point high above Geyser Hill in the Upper Geyser Basin. Starting at the footbridge across the Firehole River near Old Faithful Geyser, the trail ascends the Mallard Lake lava flow to a spectacular overview of the valley below. After the 20-30 minute climb, you can watch geysers erupt from afar, marvel at the beauty of the Old Faithful Inn, or enjoy a moment of solitude. The loop trail continues past Solitary Geyser, which erupts in small but frequent bursts.

Dr. Jake Lowenstern
US Geological Survey
Scientist-in-Charge,
Yellowstone Volcano
Observatory

Left to right: *Morning Glory Pool, Grand Prismatic Spring*

NPS Photo by Jim Peaco

on backcountry trails and boardwalks. Cyclists should wear recommended safety gear, including a helmet. Roads are narrow and drivers can be distracted. For regulations, access www.nps.gov/yell. The following routes in Old Faithful Area are restricted to bicycle and foot travel (for a map of park biking routes, go online to www.nps.gov/yell):

- **Fountain Freight Road**, 6 miles north of Old Faithful. Mountain bikes recommended (5.5 miles).
- **Daisy Geyser Cut-off** to Grand Loop Road, south of Biscuit Basin (1 mile).
- The paved trail in front of **Old Faithful Inn to Morning Glory Pool**. Bicycles are not allowed on the unpaved trail continuing beyond Morning Glory Pool to Biscuit Basin (1.4 miles).
- **Lone Star Geyser Trail** – (south of Kepler Cascades' pullout) from Grand Loop Road to Lone Star Geyser (2.4 miles). Cyclists must dismount at the end of the asphalt and walk the last few hundred feet to the geyser.

Children's Activities — The **Junior Ranger Program** welcomes children ages 5-12. Upon arrival, ask for details at any visitor center. For the **Young Scientist Program**, purchase a self-guided booklet at the **Old Faithful Visitor Education Center** (for ages 5 and up; Canyon Visitor Center for 10 and older). Kids participate in activities in the visitor center and in the field. The Young Scientist Program is funded in part by the National Science Foundation through a grant to the Yellowstone Park Foundation.

Exhibits — The **Old Faithful Visitor Education Center** has interactive exhibits about hydrothermal features that actively engage the visitor in the educational process (see p38).

Fishing — Among places to fish in the Old Faithful area is **Goose Lake**, located in the Lower Geyser Basin. The lake is situated along the Fairy Falls Trail south of Fountain Flat Drive. Nearby **Firehole River** is also popular for trout fishing, as is Nez Perce Creek. Young anglers should fish the Firehole River at picnic areas.

Hiking — Always carry rain gear, extra food and water and emergency equipment when venturing into the backcountry. Obtain current trail conditions and bear activity information at the visitor center. Here are two suggested hikes in the Old Faithful Area, one easy and one moderate:

- **Lone Star Geyser**
Distance, round trip: 4.8 miles (7.7 km)
Difficulty: easy
Trailhead: 3.5 miles (5.6 km) south of Old Faithful Junction, just beyond parking for Kepler Cascades. This partially paved

trail traces an old service road beside the **Firehole River** to the Lone Star Geyser. Lone Star erupts up to 45 feet (13.7 m) from a 12-foot (3.6 m) cone approximately every 3 hours.

• **Howard Eaton**
Distance, round trip: 5.8 miles (9.3 km)
Difficulty: moderate
Trailhead: Park near Old Faithful Ranger Station. Follow the paved path across Grand Loop Road. Turn left at the first intersection, turn left again, and follow orange trail markers to the beginning of the trail. The trail climbs a burned hill, continues through spruce-fir forest, then heads down to Lone Star Geyser. Return the same way that you came.

Programs/Outings — Ranger Programs at **Old Faithful Visitor Education Center** are held late May to late September, and usually include short **guided walks, interactive programs, geyser watches**, and in the Visitor Center theater, 45min **illustrated programs** in the evening. Check the park's newspaper distributed at the entrance gate when you arrive for more information about Ranger Programs. **Photo Safaris**, organized by Xanterra and offered at Old Faithful Inn, take shutterbugs on a photographer-guided outing to shoot the wildlife and landscapes of the area. Inquire at the front desk of any lodging in the Yellowstone area.

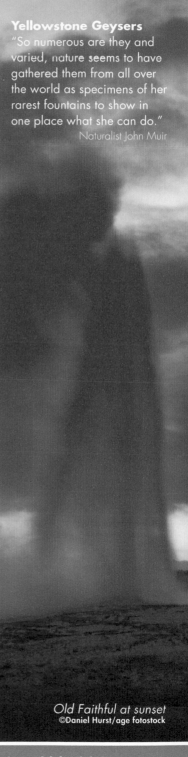

Yellowstone Geysers
"So numerous are they and varied, nature seems to have gathered them from all over the world as specimens of her rarest fountains to show in one place what she can do."
Naturalist John Muir

Old Faithful at sunset
©Daniel Hurst/age fotostock

Tours — Park-guided tours: Old Faithful Inn Tour is given, free of charge, several times daily in summer. Meet by the fireplace in the lobby to learn about the history of this hostelry and about its architect, Robert Reamer. **Guide-accompanied tours** by authorized outfitters are available. For information, call 307-344-7381, or visit www.nps.gov.yell. **Private Custom Tours** are also available: touring itineraries tailored to your preferences include pick up and drop off in-park or out of park. Touring vehicles range from 4 passenger autos and 12-passenger vans to the park's historic 13-passenger **Yellow Buses** and 36-passenger buses. Stop by the activities desk or call 307-344-7311 for reservations.

Winter

Courses/Outings — Xanterra Parks & Resorts offers activities for guests and park visitors. www.nps.gov/yell. Outings usually include **cross-country skiing** and **snowshoeing** (*see www.YellowstoneNationalParkLodges.com*).

Snowcoach Tours: Full and half-day interpretive tours in heated over-snow vehicles serve Old Faithful. These tours also act as winter transportation.

Ski and Snowshoe Tours: Half and full days outings are available.

To reserve any of these tours, call 307-344-7311 or toll-free 1-866-439-7375, or visit the front desk at **Old Faithful Snow Lodge**.

Tours are also available from Mammoth Hot Springs Hotel. For more information on winter activities, access www.nps.gov/yell.

Weather permitting, an **ice-skating rink** is open in the winter season. No reservations are necessary. Skate rentals are available through the front desk at **Old Faithful Snow Lodge**.

DRIVE
Firehole Lake Drive★

A quiet 3-mile, one-way circuit east of the Grand Loop Road, this route winds past **Great Fountain Geyser★★**, the **White Dome** and **Pink Cone** geysers, and **Firehole Lake**, with runoff in every direction. Between Great Fountain's 45-60min eruptions at intervals of 8-12hrs, the still water of its broad, circular pool mirrors the sky in myriad terraces. This geyser reserves its rare "superburst," with heights of 200ft or more, for only the most fortunate of Yellowstone visitors. Firehole Lake's thermal waters flow through the forest here, giving trees a skeletal appearance of stark white stockings and gray trunks. The absorption of sinter (dissolved minerals) kills the trees but acts as a preservative, delaying their decay.

SHOP

(*see Shopping p84*)
Bookstore, Old Faithful Visitor
Education Center
Gift Shop, Old Faithful Inn
Lower General Store
Upper General Store
Gift Shop, Old Faithful Snow
Lodge
Gift Shop, Old Faithful Lodge.

EAT

(*see Eating in the Park p87*)
Bear Paw Deli
Cafeteria at Old Faithful Lodge
Geyser Grill
Snack Shop at Old Faithful
Lodge
Obsidian Restaurant in Old
Faithful Snow Lodge
Old Faithful Inn Dining Room
Picnic Areas – East Lot,
Spring Creek and Delacey
Creek Picnic Areas.

STAY

(*see Overnighting in the Park p90*)
Old Faithful Inn
Old Faithful Lodge
Old Faithful Snow Lodge.

**INSIDER TIP
FISHING**

🐾 Nowhere in the world are
there so many public rivers,
lakes and streams found
in such a small area as in
Yellowstone. An important
mistake is trying to fish too
much too quickly, however.
First, learn about a few
rivers, lakes and streams in
Yellowstone before setting off
to fish them. You will catch
more fish, use less gasoline,
be less frustrated and enjoy the
total Yellowstone experience
far more because of it.
Seven varieties of game
fish live in the park: brook,
brown, cutthroat, lake and
rainbow trout, along with
grayling and whitefish.
There is fishing for the whole
family in the park. Willing
brook trout and grayling
can be counted on to come
to flies for **beginning
anglers** on rivers like the
Gardner and small streams
such as **Indian-Panther
and Straight Creeks**,
and **Grebe Lake**. Hard to
fool, selective brown-rainbow
and cutthroat trout are a
challenge for serious veteran
anglers on rivers like the
**Madison, Lewis, Lamar
and Slough Creek**.
                    Craig Mathews
Nationally recognized
fly-fishing guide, Blue Ribbon
Flies, West Yellowstone

Old Faithful Visitor Education Center

Yellowstone National Park's newest learning facility has been described as a "cathedral to the temple of nature." The 26,000sq ft building opened in August 2010, and was among the first visitor centers in the National Park system to earn the US Green Building Council's Gold LEED (Leadership in Energy and Environmental Design) Certification. It replaced a smaller center located here since 1971. The design of the building mimics nature and the architecture of the surrounding historic buildings. **Its pitched roofs mirror the area's mountain peaks**; other exterior features nod to nearby Old Faithful Inn and the other "parkitecture" of Yellowstone. Inside, a bright and spacious grand **entrance hall** leads directly to the center's focal point: a 36ft wall of glass panes that frames a view of the world-famous Old Faithful Geyser, 200 yards away. The center's 4,500sq ft of exhibit space is designed to provide visitors with highly accessible explanations of the science behind the park's hydrothermal features. Engaging touch-screen exhibits explain the park's most fascinating natural features such as Morning Glory Pool and Mud Volcano. The **Young Scientist room** includes an enclosed ceiling-high geyser model. Other features include a life-size **wildlife habitat** and a video screen with a realistic look into the mouth of a mudpot. A large theater provides a venue for films and ranger-led talks. Near the south entrance to the main hall, a **bookstore** is operated by the Yellowstone Association.

Nearly all of the construction waste from the new center, more than 540 tons, was either recycled or salvaged. The floors and exhibit materials are made from renewable materials. Its shallow foundation does not interfere with the thermal activity below ground that produces the magnificent natural attractions outside.

The **Yellowstone Park Foundation** raised $15 million in private contributions for the highly anticipated facility, which was matched by $12 million in federal funds.

©Gwen Cannon/Michelin

INSIDER TIP
HOT WATER

🐾 Many people who visit Yellowstone National Park ask, "Is the geyser water really hot?" and the answer to that question is an unqualified YES. Please do not be tempted to touch the water any time you are near a thermal area. And remember to keep your pets from coming into contact with the thermal water as well. A paw or a nose is just as much at risk of being severely burned as your fingers and toes.

While in the park, pets must be leashed. Pets are prohibited on trails, in the backcountry, and in thermal basins. They are not allowed more than 100 feet from a road or parking area. For details, see www.nps.gov/yell.

Suzanne Lewis
Former Yellowstone National Park Superintendent (retired)

Top to bottom, Old Faithful Visitor Education Center: *Lobby, Wildlife habitat exhibit, Entrance to Young Scientist room, Exhibit hall*

North of Old Faithful, along the Grand Loop Road, Mother Nature continues her primordial display of geological theater, intermittently hissing, bubbling, snorting and steaming amid stretches of dramatic mountain peaks, canyons, valleys, waterfalls and cascades.

Lying 14 miles east of the park's West Entrance, Madison sits near three rivers: the Firehole and the Gibbon, which converge to create the namesake Madison, which is one of the three forks forming the Missouri River. A hub of human activity, Madison has an information station, a junior ranger station and a museum. Activities here range from hiking to camping and picnicking. Located 14 miles northeast of Madison, Norris is home to the Norris Geyser Basin Museum and Information Station.

SEE
See map inside front cover.
West Entrance Road
The heaviest traffic into the park comes through the West Entrance Road (US 20), which parallels the Madison River as it heads east toward Madison. About 10 miles from the entrance and on the right, the **Mount Haynes Overlook** provides a picture-perfect view of the mountain's asymmetrical 8,235ft tall peak.

Visitors entering the area from the south via the Grand Loop Road can take a worthwhile detour along **Firehole Canyon Drive** (*see Drive below*).

Madison Junction
Located at the confluence of the **Gibbon and Firehole Rivers** where the **Madison River** forms, Madison Junction is best known in stories as the spot where the national park concept was born. Legend has it that a campfire chat in 1870, after members of the Washburn Expedition explored much of what today is Yellowstone National Park, ignited the idea.

Below: *Madison River*

NPS Photo by Jim Peaco

Hot Springs

Just north of Madison, past trails leading to **Purple Mountain**, a flat-topped ridge made of purple rock six miles wide, a **boardwalk** provides a short (one-third mile), rewarding tour of several hot springs. Among them are **Bath Spring** and **Terrace Spring**, where water appears to be boiling, but the cause is actually carbon dioxide bubbling to the surface.

Gibbon Falls

Farther north, up the Gibbon River, **Gibbon Falls** tumbles 84ft in a gradual descent over remnants of the Yellowstone Caldera rim. A trail with **overlooks** offers scenic **views**★★ of the lacy ribbon-like falls.

Artist Paint Pots

Here iron oxide stains white mud, leaving an artist's palette of pastel colors at this small and often overlooked site. Along a one-mile **loop trail**, visitors can count the number of different hues of the hot springs, listen to the gurgle and plop of two large **mudpots**, and walk through a section of forest burned in the 1988 fires.

Chocolate Pots

Positioned along the Gibbon River between Elk Park and Gibbon Meadow, these rich, brown-colored pots, roiling at a steamy temperature of 130°F, are home to warmth-loving

INSIDER TIP
VOLCANIC LEGACY

🐾 To a geologist, evidence of Yellowstone's fiery past is everywhere. As you travel along the road from Gibbon Falls to Madison Junction, you'll see cliffs of welded fragments of pumice, ash and rock on your right that testify to the cataclysmic formation of the Yellowstone Caldera some 640,000 years ago. Farther along, you'll pass Terrace Spring, CO_2 charged water that gushes out of the caldera wall. To your left are the younger lava flows that erupted more peacefully, filling the caldera with new rock and evening out its rugged topography. The Gibbon River meanders its way through the "moat" between the caldera wall and the younger lavas. Like most streams in the caldera, it maneuvers through the cracks and valleys left behind after volcanic activity.

Dr. Jake Lowenstern
US Geological Survey
Scientist-in-Charge, Yellowstone Volcano Observatory

bacteria and algae. Ferric oxide causes the striking orange-brown hue along the sides of the cones.

Norris Geyser Basin★★

Active for more than 100,000 years, this basin is one of the oldest and hottest thermal areas in the park, as well as its most dynamic. The highest hydrothermal temperature ever recorded in the park, 459°F, was in Norris, where a test hole drilled into the basin hit a depth of 1,087ft. Loop trails divide the area into two parts, Back Basin and Porcelain Basin, where more than 180 features reside. The major geysers can be found in **Back Basin★**, where thermal features are scattered among the trees. **Steamboat Geyser** is the world's tallest active geyser. Its rare major eruptions (it is dormant for years at a time) can reach heights of 400ft. **Echinus Geyser**, the largest acid-water geyser, used to put on an entertaining show every 40-80 minutes erupting and draining like a toilet bowl. However, in recent times, the geyser erupts irregularly, and can rest for months without an eruption. It's best to check with a ranger at nearby Norris Museum for up-to-date information.
Porcelain Basin, named for its milky white, mineral-rich water is home to **Constant Geyser**, which erupts about every 20 minutes, spewing water as high as 30ft. The green-rimmed **Whirligig Geyser**

sprays water in unpredictable directions. The area also includes the **Black Growler Steam Vent**, a noisy steam column, and Crackling Lake, named for the popping sounds it makes along its southern edge. Deep blue water with a yellow sulfuric lining combine to form **Emerald Spring** nearby. Entering the Norris Geyser Basin from the Grand Loop, the **Norris Geyser Basin Museum** (*see Museums below*) provides a scenic gateway for visitors to Porcelain Basin through its central breezeway.

Virginia Cascade

Some 2.5mi east of Norris Junction, a steep, curvy spur road coming off the main road provides several views of the Gibbon River's stunning 60ft plunge over volcanic rock. Parking is difficult due to the narrowness of the road.

Fire Exhibit

"Tonight, this is all that's left of Yellowstone," reported a famous journalist in 1988 from the site of the Norris-Canyon blowdown, a 22-mile stretch where lodgepole pines were felled in 1984 by a massive windstorm and burned four years later in the park's epic fire. An exhibit on the south side of the road about 3.5mi east of Norris tells the story. But the area today shows evidence of continuing regrowth.

Roaring Mountain

Five miles north of Norris Geyser Basin, this 8,152ft acidic thermal area is covered with fumaroles on its western slope. During the park's early years, the hissing steam could reportedly be heard for miles. Steam still rises from the slope, most visible on cold days. The acidic soil keeps the ground here devoid of brush and plant life.

NPS Photo by Jim Peaco

Obsidian Cliff

Native Americans quarried materials from the base of this cliff, located north of Roaring Mountain. The early inhabitants of Yellowstone placed such a high value on obsidian for tools and weapons that it was traded as far away as Mexico and Guatemala. It is illegal to remove archaeological artifacts from the park. Please observe them, and report their location to a park ranger so that others can enjoy them as well.

NPS Photo by Jim Peaco

DO

Check www.nps.gov/yell and www.YellowstoneNationalPark Lodges.com for current fees and schedules for the activities and programs that follow.

YPF Photo by Tom Porter

Top to bottom: *Aerial view of Obsidian Cliff, Back Basin, Norris Geyser Basin*

Aquatic Invasive Species
The introduction of foreign parasites to Yellowstone's waterways is an increasing threat. These dangerous hitchhikers disrupt the ecosystem. The whirling disease parasite attacks the cartilage of fish and inhibits their ability to feed. Recent studies have shown that it is spreading quickly among the cutthroat trout population in Yellowstone Lake. The New Zealand mud snail attaches to boats and gear and devours vital aquatic insects. Anglers are required to thoroughly clean mud, plants and debris from all gear before arriving in the park and before entering another park waterbody. Anglers should drain boats, and clean fish near the same water in which they were caught. Minnows, leeches, salamanders and other types of bait are prohibited in the park.

Summer
Biking – If cycling in Yellowstone in late summer or early autumn, know that:

Left to right: *Artist Paint Pots, Emerald Spring*

- The weather is unpredictable, and severe winter conditions can be encountered at any time. Roads may have snow and ice.
- Bring food, water, extra clothing, and a bicycle repair kit.
- Water is available *only* at the **Madison Picnic Area** and Mammoth.
- Ride single file to the right. Be aware that most park roads have very narrow shoulders.
- Wear a helmet and high visibility clothing.
- Night rides are not advised.
- See park routes open to bicycles at this time of year at www.nps.gov/yell.

Biking is permitted on the following route in the **West Entrance Area** (for a **map of all biking routes** in the park, visit www.nps.gov/yell).
Riverside Trail from Boundary Street trailhead (in West Yellowstone) to Barnes Road (1.4 miles).

Children's Activities – The **Junior Ranger Station**

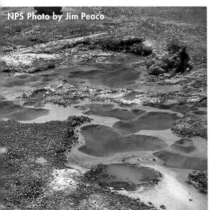

NPS Photo by Jim Peaco

NPS Photo by Jim Peaco

located in the historic Madison Information Station at Madison Junction offers park activities, usually in 30-minute time periods during the summer, for children ages 5 to12. If they complete the ranger-led requirements, they can earn a Junior Ranger patch. Meet at the Junior Ranger Station.

Exhibits – Built between 1929 and 1930, the **Norris Geyser Basin Museum** is a National Historic Landmark. Located in Norris, it is one of the park's original trailside museums. Framed with massive logs, it is constructed of wood and stone. Inside, touch-table exhibits explain hydrothermal geology, the history of the Norris Geyser Basin and thermal area plant and animal life. Plans are underway to install orientation panels. A bookstore also occupies the premises.

The **Museum of the National Park Ranger** is situated just north of Norris, on the east side of the Grand Loop Road. This former station for soldiers who patrolled the basin suffered a fire in 1897 and an earthquake in 1959. Restored in 1991, the building houses exhibits on the ranger profession in this erstwhile early 20C army outpost.

Fishing – Firehole Cascades, well-known among anglers, can be found just before Firehole Canyon Drive rejoins the Grand Loop Road.

**INSIDER TIP
PARK MUSEUMS**

🐾 Though some say that the other "Y" park—Yosemite— was the first national park (established as a California state park 18 years *before* the creation of Yellowstone National Park, and as national park 18 years *after* Yellowstone), Yosemite did boast the first full-fledged educational museum. In 1924 the Laura Spelman Rockefeller Memorial granted money to Yosemite for a museum. Yellowstone's superintendent Horace Albright wrote the interior secretary, urging him to "got a piece of the pie for Yellowstone." Money began to trickle Yellowstone's way from the memorial in 1928, enough to break ground for four roadside museums. They were needed to teach the public about park resources, but most importantly, education led to respect. Today, park visitors can experience these early museums at Madison, Norris, and Fishing Bridge. The museum buildings were designed by architect Herbert Maier during the National Park Service Rustic Architecture period (1917-1937).

**Karen Reinhart
Author**, *Old Faithful Inn: Crown Jewel of National Park Lodges*, **and** *Yellowstone's Rebirth by Fire: Rising from the Ashes of the 1988 Fires*

The **Firehole River** is one of the most highly favored streams in the park. Initiating south of the Old Faithful Area, the Firehole flows north to join the Gibbon River and form the Madison River. Its waters are famed for rainbow, brown and brook trout. There is a **fishing ramp and a platform** at the Mount Haynes Overlook, about 3.5 miles (5.6km) west of Madison Junction. Fishing the **Madison River** is permitted; fly fishing is popular on this waterway. Two places ideal for young anglers are the **Gibbon River** near Tuff Cliffs (Madison area) and Virginia Meadows (Norris area) and **Solfatara Creek** near Norris Campground.

Hiking – Here are two suggested hikes in the Madison-Norris Area, one easy and one moderate.

• **Harlequin Lake**
Distance, round trip: 1 mile (1.6 km)

Difficulty: easy
Trailhead: 1.5 miles west of Madison Campground on the West Entrance road. This hike is a gentle ascent through burned lodgepole pines to a small, marshy lake frequented by waterfowl (but not harlequin ducks).

• **Purple Mountain**
Distance, round trip: 6 miles (10 km)
Difficulty: Moderate, with a climb of 1,500 feet
Trailhead: 1/4 mile north of Madison Junction on the Madison-Norris road; limited parking. This trail ascends through intermittent burned lodgepole pine forest and ends with a view of the Firehole Valley and lower Gibbon Valley; some views of the Madison Junction area are also visible.

Programs/Outings –
Madison Evening Program: each night during the summer, a park ranger gives a 45min illustrated program on Yellowstone's wonders.

Below: *Winter, Firehole Falls*

NPS Photo by Jim Peaco

Check the local bulletin boards or inquire at the **Madison Information Station**. Meet at the Madison Amphitheater. Ranger-guided **walks** in the Norris hydrothermal area last about 1.5hrs. The summer **Norris Campfire Program:** 45min campfire talks by a ranger.

Watch the local bulletin boards for program notices. Meet at the Norris Campground Campfire Circle.

Wildlife Viewing – The **Madison River**, particularly from the West Entrance to Madison, plays hosts to **trumpeter swans**, which can be seen along the riverbanks in summer. Canadian geese also frequent these waters. Please remember that it is illegal to feed wildlife. All visitors must keep 100 yards from wolves and bears, and 25 yards from other animals.

DRIVE
Firehole Canyon Drive
Visitors entering the Madison-Norris Area from the south via Grand Loop Road can take the worthwhile detour along **Firehole Canyon Drive**, which is a 2-mile one-way road just before Madison Junction. The drive offers outstanding views of **Firehole Falls**. Near the end of this road is an unstaffed swimming hole, popular during summer months, with restrooms that double as a changing area. It is one

of only two legal swimming areas in the park. Cliff diving is strictly prohibited, however. The **Firehole Cascades** can be seen just before Firehole Canyon Drive reconnects with the Grand Loop Road.

SHOP
(see Shopping p84)
Bookstores in the Norris Geyser Basin Museum and Madison Information Station.

EAT
(see Eating in the Park p87)
Madison Picnic Areas – One picnic area lies along the Madison River about midway between the West Entrance and Madison. The second area is located at Madison Junction. A short drive north of Madison Junction is the **Tuff Cliff Picnic Area**. Along the Gibbon River between Madison and Norris, **Gibbon Meadows Picnic Area** sits northwest of the Artists Paint Pots. **Norris Meadows Picnic Area** sits just east of Norris.

STAY
(see Overnighting in the Park p90)
Madison Campground – This large campground stretches out near the confluence of the three rivers.
Norris Campground – This campground is located about 0.8 mile (1.3 km) north of Norris Junction.

Occupying the northwest corner of the park, Mammoth is Yellowstone's command post. Its eastern anchors are the park's North Entrance at Gardiner, Montana, and Norris to the south. With multicolored terraces perched on a hillside above it, the park's headquarters are located among the area's historic buildings. The green lawns and orderly appearance recall Mammoth's early history as an Army post. But the star of the show is Mammoth Hot Springs and those magnificent travertine terraces, eerily beautiful in winter, too, when snowshoeing and skiing are popular here.

SEE
See map inside front cover

Roosevelt Arch
The North Entrance Road into Yellowstone from Gardiner, Montana was the first major entrance to the park and is the only entrance that remains plowed throughout the year. Here, the 50ft-high **Roosevelt Arch** stands as an enduring symbol of Yellowstone, first welcoming visitors arriving by stagecoach from Gardiner until 1915, when automobiles were permitted into the park. In April 1903 the arch's namesake, President **Theodore Roosevelt**, dedicated the immense stone arch. **Robert Reamer**, architect of the Old Faithful Inn, may have contributed to the design. Inscribed along the top are words from the Act of Congress that set aside this land "For the Benefit and Enjoyment of the People."

Yellowstone Heritage and Research Center
Within view of the Roosevelt Arch at the North Entrance, this center in Gardiner houses one of the National Park Service's most comprehensive collections of historical documents and photos, artifacts and natural specimens.

Left to right: *Mammoth terraces; sunrise, Swan Lake*

YPF Photo by Tom Porter

he three-story building, opened
n 2005, is climate-controlled
o preserve more than five
million items. Among them
are Thomas Moran's original
watercolors and William Henry
Jackson's photos. Public tours
of the archives and museum
collection are by appointment
only (*Jun–early Sept*). Space is
limited to 10 participants; call
307-344-2662 for reservations.
The library is open to the public
Tue–Thu.

Boiling River

A parking area on the road's
east side provides access to a
half-mile trail leading to **Boiling
River**, where swimming is
permitted during daylight,
normally beginning mid-summer.
Here, hydrothermally heated
water warms a stretch of
the **Gardner River**. Elk,
pronghorn, deer and bison can
be spotted in the canyon near
crumbling walls of sandstone
and prehistoric mudflows along
the road to Mammoth.

Fort Yellowstone

Topped with red roofs and
numerous chimneys, several
buildings, many of stone, remain
from Fort Yellowstone, which
was built by the US Calvary in
the 1890s and early 1900s.
Today they house administration
staff and the **Horace M.
Albright Visitor Center
and Museum**★★ (*see Exhibits
below*). The facility also serves
as a Yellowstone information
center and backcountry permit
office. The single public
building along the road to
Tower-Roosevelt is **Mammoth
Chapel**, the final structure built
by the army in Mammoth in
1913. Open for worship and
weddings, the recently restored
chapel features a vestibule with
stained-glass windows depicting
scenes of Old Faithful and the
Lower Falls of the Yellowstone.
A self-guided walking tour
brochure on the fort buildings is
available at the visitor center.

NPS Photo

Mammoth Hot Springs★★★

Change, constant throughout Yellowstone, is most obvious at Mammoth Hot Springs. Each day, two tons of travertine are deposited by the relatively cool (170°F) hot springs. Local hydrothermal water reacts with the area's limestone bedrock, creating a solution rich in dissolved calcium carbonate. As this solution reaches the surface, the decreasing pressure causes carbon dioxide gas to bubble out (as in a freshly opened bottle of soda). The loss of gas causes the water to form deposits of travertine, a variety of calcium carbonate similar to the deep limestone. Brilliant color is added to this three-dimensional "canvas" by algae and tiny living bacteria. Impressive from a distance, this formation is truly remarkable when viewed up close, where the elaborate collection of minute cascades and multicolored terraces resemble a still photo of a waterfall.

Elevated boardwalks climb and descend the ornate flows of the Main Terrace, popular with elk, which recline here like living sculptures. Hydrothermal features like **Minerva Spring★★★** and **Opal Terrace★★** are constantly changing, and activity varies from year to year.

A couple of hundred yards north, the distinctive **Liberty Cap★** juts from the earth like a massive Christmas tree. This extinct hot-spring cone was named for its resemblance to the hats worn by colonial patriots. The **Upper Terrace Overlook** provides a comprehensive **view** of the entire Mammoth Hot Springs area. **Canary Spring,** on the far edge of the Lower Terraces, excites observers with its brilliant yellow hue and considerable heat. As large amounts of water stream down to the terraces below, the terrace continues to grow, and the boardwalk has to be moved.

Mammoth Hot Springs Hotel

(*see Stay below*) The most interesting aspect of this nearby hotel is a US map near the lobby. Assembled on a wall like a large puzzle, it features states that are carefully cut from 15 different woods from 9 countries.

The Hoodoos

About two miles south from the turnoff to Upper Terrace Loop Drive stands a massive jumble of travertine rocks on the side of the road. Their unusual name refers to the bizarre appearance of the sharp sedimentary rocks that slid from the slopes of Terrace Mountain to the west.

Mount Everts

This prominent 7,831ft peak due east of Mammoth is named for **Truman C. Everts**, a member of the 1870 Washburn Expedition. Everts spent 37 days wandering the forest after being

separated from his camping party. His lost-in-the-wilderness story of starvation, hypothermia and hallucinations is one of Yellowstone's best-known survival tales. Four miles southeast of Mammoth, **Lava Creek** (*see Hiking below*) spills over a cliff of basalt lava flow at Undine Falls, a multi-drop waterfall cascading down some 100ft. Less than a mile from the road, **Wraith Falls** (*see Hiking below*) to the east drops about 100ft of cold, frothy water from Lupine Creek.

©Edgloris E. Marys/age fotostock

Bunsen Peak

Named for **Robert Wilhelm Bunsen**, the German physicist and geyser researcher who also inspired the Bunsen burner, this 8,564ft volcanic peak dominates the southern horizon of Mammoth. A hiking trail leading to the top begins 5 miles south of Mammoth.

To the south, scenic **Swan Lake** occasionally plays host to trumpeter swans. Wolves are often sighted on nearby **Swan Lake Flat**. To the east along the roadside, **Rustic Falls** draws water from Glen Creek. These falls plunge 47ft over volcanic rock and are worth the stop for a roadside view. To the east but not visible from the road, **Osprey Falls** plunges 150ft into a spectacular canyon.

Top to bottom: *Travertine pool ledges at Mammoth main terrace, Mammoth upper terraces*

YPF Photo by Tom Porter

Apollinaris Spring

South of Mammoth this natural spring is an historic site, where in 1925, limestone slabs were laid to pave a path to obsidian and granite boulders carefully stacked around a cold-water spring. In 2006 the Yellowstone Park Foundation funded the restoration of this natural and cultural treasure.

DO

Check www.nps.gov/yell and www.YellowstoneNationalPark Lodges.com for current fees and schedules.

Summer

Biking – Several gravel roads are open to both bicycle and automotive traffic. The Old Gardiner Road allows two-way bike traffic and one-way auto traffic. The road is best suited for **mountain bikes**.
The following routes in Mammoth are restricted to bicycle and foot travel only (for a **map of biking routes** in the park, visit www.nps.gov/yell):

- Abandoned railroad bed paralleling **Yellowstone River between Gardner and the park boundary at Reese Creek** (5 miles).
- **Bunsen Peak Road** to a Mammoth housing and maintenance area (6 miles).

Children's Activities – The **Junior Ranger Program** is open to children ages 5-12. Some winter activities require the use of a thermometer and hand lens, so make sure you ask to check out a Junior Ranger Snowpack, which is available at Mammoth's **Albright Visitor Center**; **snowshoes** may be checked out in Mammoth. For details, go online to www.nps.gov/yell.

Exhibits – The **museum** in the **Horace M. Albright Visitor Center** traces the human and natural history of the park, highlighting Thomas Moran paintings and William Henry Jackson photographs from the 1871 Hayden expedition. Upstairs are exhibits relating to a predator-prey theme. The visitor center's theater shows films about Yellowstone on the half hour in summer and on request in winter.

Fishing – Fishing along the **Gardner River** is popular in the Mammoth Area. Full-day **Fly Fishing Guide** service is available daily from Mammoth in summer. In the form of a walk-wade experience (no float tubes), the service includes in-park transportation to fishing areas, flies, lunch and soft drinks. Fly rods and waders are available to rent. A Yellowstone Park fishing permit is required. A Fly Fishing Gear Package is available per person per day. Other fine fishing holes, especially for youngsters, include **Blacktail Deer Creek, Joffe Lake**, and **Indian Creek** near the campground of the same name.

Hiking – Always carry rain gear, extra food and water and emergency equipment when venturing into the backcountry. Obtain current trail condition and bear activity information at the visitor center. Here are two suggested hikes:

• **Wraith Falls**
Distance, round trip: 1 mile (1.6 km)
Difficulty: easy
Trailhead: Pullout ¼ mile east of Lava Creek Picnic area on the Mammoth-Tower Road. This is a short, easy hike through open sagebrush and Douglas-fir forest to the foot of the Wraith Falls cascade on Lupine Creek.

• **Lava Creek Trail**
Round trip: 7 miles (11.3 km)
Difficulty: moderate
Trailhead: The bridge at Lava Creek Picnic Area on the Mammoth-Tower Road. This trail follows Lava Creek downstream past Undine Falls (50 feet), descending gradually. Lava Creek meets the Gardner River farther downstream. The trail crosses a foot bridge on the Gardner River, and there is one final ascent to a pullout on the North Entrance Road just north of the Mammoth Campground.

Horseback Riding – In summer Xanterra Parks & Resorts offers one-hour horseback rides along the trail below Bunsen Peak. These trail rides are available throughout the day at **Mammoth Corral**, located

less than a mile from Mammoth Hotel. Riders must be at least 8 years old, 48 inches tall, and weigh less than 240 lbs. Ages 8 through Adult. Advance reservations are required; call 307-344-7311 or 866-439-7375 for schedules and prices.

Programs/Outings – **Ranger Programs** at **Mammoth's Albright Visitor Center** are held daily year-round, and usually include **ranger talks, evening illustrated programs**, and wintertime **snowshoe walks**. Check at the visitor center or Mammoth Hotel for more information about these programs.

Tours – The park's historic 13-passenger **Yellow Buses** depart from Mammoth Hot Springs Hotel for tours. Stop by the hotel activities desk or call 307-344-7311 for information and reservations. Specific tours include **Evening Wildlife Encounters**. Given that Mammoth is prime territory for a variety of animals, early evening is an optimum time to view wildlife from a park Yellow Bus. Listen to the tour guide's tales of bygone days while you enjoy a nostalgic ride onboard this classic touring car; daily departures in summer from Mammoth Hotel. **Yellowstone in a Day** departs from Gardiner, MT and Mammoth Hotel for a tour of the entire park in one day. Please call

307-344-7311 for information, cost and reservations. Wake Up to Wildlife tour of **Lamar Valley's** spectacular scenery and animals is available in summer; tours depart daily in the early morning from Mammoth Hotel.

Wildlife Viewing – Wolves are frequently seen on **Swan Lake Flat**. Bighorn sheep claim the high reaches of **Gardner Canyon**. Among the **birds** in the area, watch along the streams especially for bald eagles, ospreys, kingfishers and the dipper, the latter a year-round park resident that sometimes moves submersed in the streambeds. *See also Winter wildlife viewing below.* Remember that **feeding animals is prohibited** in the park, and all visitors must keep 100 yards away from wolves and bears, and 25 yards from other animals.

Left to right: *Historic Yellow Bus, Bighorn sheep*

Winter
Children's Activities – Snowshoeing - See Junior Ranger Program above.

Courses/Outings – **Xanterra Parks & Resorts** offers activities for their guests and other park visitors. Outings usually include **cross-country skiing** and **snowshoeing**. Full and half-day interpretive **snowcoach tours** in heated over-the-snow vehicles are available in the Mammoth Hot Springs Area.
These tours also serve as winter transportation. **Ski and snowshoe tours**: Half and full days outings are available. For reservations and current fees, call 307-344-7311 or go online to www.Yellowstone NationalParkLodges.com.
Ice skating at Mammoth Hot Springs Hotel is available during the winter season.
An **ice-skating rink** is open depending upon the weather. No reservations are taken. Skate rentals are free and available

©Gwen Cannon/Michelin

through the front desk of Mammoth Hot Springs Hotel.

Wildlife Viewing – Gardner Canyon is a chosen wintering spot for bighorn sheep, elk and pronghorn. Keep your eyes on the cliffs above the **Gardner River** for the climbing sheep.

DRIVE
Upper Terrace Loop Drive

Drive about a half a mile from Mammoth Hotel to the boardwalks at the base of the **Terraces** and follow them to the thermal features at the top. Or drive to the top and park to explore on foot from there. The Upper Terrace Loop Drive is a short and picturesque one-way drive from the parking lot.

SHOP
(see Shopping p84)
Bookstore in Albright Visitor Center
"For Future Generations," gift shop in Mammoth Hot Springs Hotel General Store.

Wildlife Jams
Yellowstone is famed for the fact that visitors can view wild animals from their cars, but safety hazards result when cars stop in the middle of the road. If animals are present near the road, pull off to the shoulder to watch. If there isn't an adequate shoulder, drive ahead to the nearest place where there is. Every year dozens of tourists are involved in accidents caused by "wildlife jams"—rarely with serious injury, however.

EAT
(see Eating in the Park p87)
Mammoth Hot Springs Hotel Dining Room
The Terrace Grill
Picnic Areas – The Mammoth Area has 6 picnic areas (north to south): Albright, Mammoth, Wyoming/Montana State Line, Sheepeater Cliff, Apollinaris Spring and Beaver Lake.

STAY
(see Overnighting in the Park p90)
Mammoth Hot Springs Hotel and Cabins – This hotel is one of two in the park that are open in the winter season as well as in the summer season. Cabins are not open in the winter.
Camping – Open year-round, **Mammoth Campground** is located 5 miles south of the park's North Entrance. South of Mammoth Hot Springs, you'll find **Indian Creek Campground**.

NPS Photo by Jim Peaco

Yellowstone's northeastern quadrant is the park's most remote area and the best location for viewing its magnificent wildlife. The Northeast Entrance Road is considered the most scenic of the five entrances to the park due to its winding path through the elk and bison-filled Lamar Valley. This haven for wildlife (and its watchers) widens into view as the road continues west after dramatic views of the Absaroka Mountains—specifically Barronette Peak (10,404ft) to the north and Abiathar Peak (10,928ft) to the south. The full 29-mile westerly route to the quiet village of Tower-Roosevelt follows Soda Butte Creek and the Lamar River and was an important trail for American Indians, trappers and miners in the 19th century. Today, the village makes a pleasant place for a break from the crowds.

SEE

See map inside front cover.

Soda Butte

Worth a short stop along the Northeast Entrance Road to Tower-Roosevelt along Soda Butte Creek, this extinct hot spring cone made of travertine is the lone thermal feature in this area of the park.

Lamar Buffalo Ranch

Visitors are welcome to drive by to view the historic buffalo ranch, but there are no facilities open to the general public at this location.

The ranch was built in the early 1900s as part of efforts to expand the bison herd in Yellowstone. Based on the large number of bison enjoying life in the Lamar Valley in plain sight each day, it's difficult to imagine a time when these thundering ungulates were nearly eliminated from the park by poachers. Experts believe that by 1901, there were only about two-dozen bison left in Yellowstone. After the remaining animals were placed in captivity near Mammoth and protected, their numbers grew considerably and the animals were released to be raised at the ranch, where numbers reached more than 1,000 by the 1930s. It operated until the 1950s. Today,

©Philippe Clement/age fotostock

nearly 3,900 bison roam the park. The Lamar Buffalo Ranch Historic District, located about halfway through the Lamar Valley, remains home to four remaining buildings from the original compound, as well as the **Yellowstone Association Institute** and Park Service rangers who conduct courses and classes here.

Tower-Roosevelt

Sitting just west of the confluence of the Yellowstone and Lamar Rivers, this hub is regarded as one of the most relaxed villages in the park, an oasis from the other visitor-filled sections of the park. The **Tower Ranger Station** is a remodeled reconstruction of the second Tower Soldier Station built in 1907. **Roosevelt Lodge** (*see Stay below*), a rustic, one-story L-shaped lodge built in 1920, commemorates President Theodore Roosevelt's two-week visit to the park in 1903 and his reputed campsite nearby. An avid naturalist and outdoorsman, Roosevelt was one of the park's early advocates and was instrumental in the passage of a bill in 1894 protecting Yellowstone from the threat of commercial exploitation.

Petrified Tree

A mile and-a-half northwest of Tower-Roosevelt, off Grand Loop Road, this jagged redwood stump stands erect on the side of a hill near **Lost Lake Trailhead**. It was buried in volcanic ash about 50 million years ago. Easily accessible to visitors, the ancient trunk is fenced to protect its wood from collectors and vandals who chipped away at two other specimens that once stood in the area.

Specimen Ridge★

Accessible by a 2.5mi trail east of Tower Junction, this 8,442ft crest and 40sq mi of surrounding uplands

Left to right: *Lamar Valley, Bison near Soda Butte, Specimen Ridge*

NPS Photo by Jim Peaco

NPS Photo by Jim Peaco

constitute the **largest petrified forest** in the world. Remnants of more than 100 different plants, including redwoods similar to those in California, are found here. Ash and mudflows buried the trees 50 million years ago; erosion reversed the process.

Tower Fall★★

Just 2 miles southeast of Tower-Roosevelt, in the vicinity of the store, this impressive waterfall squeezes between namesake stone "towers" and plunges 132ft to join the Grand Canyon of the Yellowstone at its narrowest point. A steep **trail** (.5mi) descends 300ft to the base of the fall. The dramatic **gorge★★** is best viewed from a turnout at Calcite Springs. The **Bannock Trail,** a historic pathway used by Native Americans traveling through the area, may have passed nearby.

Calcite Springs

Smelled long before it is seen, this group of thermal springs along the Yellowstone River emits hot gases that have among the highest known concentrations of hydrogen sulfide gas in the park. The area's hydrothermally altered rhyolite inspired the artist Thomas Moran, who included a depiction of the springs among his collection of works to Congress in 1872. The steep basalt cliffs on the opposite side of the river from the overlook are remnants of an ancient lava flow. Bighorn sheep, red-tailed hawks and osprey can be spotted along the gorge and cliffs.

Lamar Valley★★

In the 1830s, an early explorer of Yellowstone, Osborne Russell, named the Lamar Valley the "Secluded Valley," a description that remains accurate today. This broad glacial valley is a highlight of any visit to Yellowstone and provides one of the park's most enduring experiences—an opportunity to witness some of the world's most majestic animals thriving in their natural habitat. Permitting wide expansive views from the Northeast Entrance Road, the valley is home to bison, elk, coyote, grizzly bears and wolves (see Wildlife Viewing below).

DO

Check www.nps.gov/yell and www.YellowstoneNationalParkLodges.com for current fees and schedules.

Summer

Biking – A gravel road open to both bicycle and automobile, **Blacktail Plateau Drive** allows two-way bike traffic and one-way auto traffic. This road is best suited for **mountain bikes**.
The following routes are restricted to bicycle and foot travel only (for a **map of biking routes** in the park, visit www.nps.gov/yell/planyourvisit):

The Wolves of Yellowstone

The reintroduction of wolves to Yellowstone after a 70-year absence is one of the great wildlife conservation success stories. By 1926, human actions had eliminated wolves from the park. In 1995 and 1996, 31 gray wolves from Canada were placed in acclimation pens in Yellowstone's Lamar Valley and gradually released into the wild. The result surprised observers across the globe. The newly arrived residents successfully formed packs and dispersed throughout the park. Currently, around 100 wolves live in Yellowstone. Research has tracked changes affecting both plants and animals throughout the entire ecosystem due to the return of this native predator.

Several programs are in place to ensure that Yellowstone's wolves continue to survive in the park. One of them is the **Wolf Collar Sponsorship** program, administered by the Yellowstone Park Foundation, which has raised $4 million in private funds to finance the continual monitoring and research of wolf packs.

The promise of catching a glimpse of these clever animals attracts thousands of visitors to the park, in all seasons, especially to the Lamar Valley.

Best times to see wolves are early in the morning or at dusk. Bring a scope or binoculars for maximum sighting.

- **Mount Washburn** from Chittenden Road parking area to summit of Mount Washburn (2.5 miles). Bicycles are not permitted on the southern trail between the summit and Dunraven Pass parking area.
- **Old Chittenden Service Road** between Grand Loop Road and Tower Fall Campground (2 miles).
- **Rose Creek Service Road** behind the Lamar Ranger Station (1 mile).

Cookouts – Old West Dinner Cookouts head out by horse-drawn wagon and horseback from Roosevelt Lodge nightly in summer. A dinner of steak, Roosevelt baked beans, potato salad, corn, cole slaw, corn muffins, watermelon and fruit crisp is served with music and storytelling.

Reserve in advance by calling Xanterra at 307-344-7311, or toll-free at 1-866-439-7375.

Fishing – The **Yellowstone River** is prime angling territory. **Slough Creek**, accessible by Slough Creek Trail off the Northeast Entrance Road, is a favorite of catch-and-release anglers from around the country. Young anglers should try **Trout Lake** or **Pebble Creek** near the campground of the same name.

Hiking – Backcountry permits and general hiking information are available from Tower Ranger Station.

- **Slough Creek Trail**
Distance, round trip:
2 miles (3.2 km) one way to First Meadow; 5 miles (8 km) one way to Second Meadow.

Difficulty: moderately strenuous for first 1.5 miles (2.4 km), then easy.

Trailhead: Near the vault toilet on the road to Slough Creek Campground. This trail follows a historic wagon trail up Slough Creek through several meadows and over Plateau and Elk Tongue creeks. From the trailhead, the trail switchbacks up a moderately steep trail and rejoins Slough Creek in about 2 miles (3.2 km) at the first meadow. Moose are commonly seen. **Grizzly and black bears** also use this valley. As on all Yellowstone trails, be alert for the possibility of bears in the backcountry.

• Lost Lake Trail
Distance, round trip: 4 miles (6.4 km).
Difficulty: moderately strenuous.
Trailhead: Behind Roosevelt Lodge. This trail climbs 300 feet (91m) onto the bench, where it joins Roosevelt horse trail (if you meet horses, move to the downhill side of the trail and remain still until they have passed) and continues west to Lost Lake. From Lost Lake, the trail follows the contour around the hillside to the Petrified Tree parking area. Cross the parking lot and climb the hill at its northeast end to loop back behind Tower Ranger Station. Cross the creek and return to the Roosevelt Lodge cabins. This excursion offers views of the lake, waterfowl, wet meadows, sagebrush hilltops, wildflowers, and often black bears.

Horseback Riding – From Roosevelt Lodge Corral in summer, daily 1hr and 2hr horseback rides are offered. Inquire at Roosevelt Lodge for details, fees and reservations. Horseback rides can be booked in advance by calling Xanterra's toll-free number: 1-866-439-7375 or 307-344-7311.

Left to right: *Blacktail Plateau, Grizzly bear*

NPS Photo by Jo Suderman

Stagecoach Rides –
Hear about the history of stage-coaches in Yellowstone during a ride in an Old West stagecoach. Stagecoarch rides are offered throughout the day during the summer season from Roosevelt Corral.

Tours – Wildlife-viewing tour of Lamar Valley's spectacular scenery and wildlife in summer. For more information and reservation, contact Xanterra at 307-344-7311, or toll-free at 1-866-439-7375.

Wildlife Viewing in Lamar Valley – The best time to observe animals is at dawn or dusk when wolves and bears may come into sight. Visitors can be found waiting in folding chairs along one of many roadside viewpoints between Slough Creek and Pebble Creek, prepared with binoculars in hand and spotting scopes at the ready to view wildlife grazing or hunting on the open hillsides.

DRIVE
Blacktail Plateau Drive
Take Grand Loop Road northwest from Tower-Roosevelt, and continue past the petrified tree and Phantom Lake. Before reaching the self-guided hiking trail, turn left onto a gravel road open for one-way auto traffic. This road continues east to rejoin Grand Loop Road.

SHOP
(*see Shopping p84*)
Roosevelt Lodge Gift Shop.

EAT
(*see Eating in the Park p87*)
Roosevelt Lodge Dining Room
Old West Dinner Cookouts
(*see Cookouts above*)
Picnic Areas in the Tower-Roosevelt Area are **Warm Creek** at the Northeast Entrance Road, and **Soda Butte** and **Yellowstone River Picnic Areas** along the Northeast Entrance Road.

STAY
(*see Overnighting in the Park p90*)
Roosevelt Lodge and Cabins
Camping – Slough Creek Campground is situated 5miles east of Tower Junction, 2.5miles down a dirt road.
Pebble Creek Campground sits 9 miles west of the Northeast Entrance.
Tower Fall Campground can be found 2 miles south of Tower Junction.

NPS Photo by Jim Peaco

Yellowstone boasts its own grand canyon: one carved by the Yellowstone River, rather than the Colorado River. With its steep golden cliffs, jagged ridges, mighty waterway and crashing falls, the area encompassing the Grand Canyon of the Yellowstone provides some of the most dazzling views in the park. Here, Mother Nature's masterwork in erosion and her past volcanic fury remain on full display. Grand Loop Road between Tower-Roosevelt and Canyon Village crosses the highest terrain accessible by car in the park (closed during winter due to snow). Its sharp, thrilling curves provide access to many fine views at roadside turnouts. South of the Canyon Village area is Hayden Valley, home to abundant wildlife easily observable from the road.

SEE

See map inside front cover.

Mount Washburn

South of Tower-Roosevelt, 10,243ft Mount Washburn rises to the east; a three-story fire tower on its peak can be seen from the road. Nearby, bighorn sheep can sometimes be spotted. A three-mile hiking trail to the summit begins at a parking area off the one-mile Chittenden Road.

Dunraven Pass★

The highest mountain pass in Yellowstone at 8,800ft, Dunraven Pass offers the park's best perspective on the contours of the ancient Yellowstone Caldera, along with spectacular **views★★** of the Absaroka and Beartooth ranges to the east. The road's twists and turns are often enjoyed by motorcyclists and driving enthusiasts, despite the 25mph speed limit. The level of difficulty, however, can prove to be a challenge for RVs.

Left to right: *Grand Canyon of the Yellowstone, Lower Falls*

©Danita Delimont Stock/age fotostock

Canyon Village

The finest viewpoints of the Grand Canyon of the Yellowstone are clustered along the junction just south of this busy village, which was once home to the Canyon Hotel, destroyed by fire in 1959. Today's **Canyon Lodge** helps accommodate the area's considerable number of park visitors.

Stop in the village at the two-story **Canyon Visitor Education Center**, which opened in 2006. In addition to offering park information to visitors, it features displays that focus on the park's geological features and volcanic history (*see Exhibits below*).

Grand Canyon of the Yellowstone★★★

After Old Faithful, this magnificent canyon is probably the park's best-known feature. The vast canyon measures roughly 20mi long, 800ft-1,200ft deep and 1,500ft-4,000ft wide. The brilliant golden-yellow color of its rhyolite rock is due to iron compounds "cooked" by hydrothermal activity. Weathering oxidation of the iron produced the yellow, orange, red and brown colors.

At the end of the last Ice Age, scientists believe ice dams formed at the mouth of Yellowstone Lake. When breached, they released tremendous amounts of water, carving the canyon. Today, steam rises from its hot springs and perpetual spouters below. Only one strenuous hiking route, the **Seven-Mile Hole Trail**, reaches the canyon floor.

Two key features of the canyon's dramatic scenery, the Yellowstone River's **Upper Falls★** and **Lower Falls★★** can be viewed along North Rim and South Rim drives (see Drive below). The 109ft Upper Falls stands at a higher elevation than its downstream neighbor. Lower Falls, at 308ft is the tallest waterfall in the park, and is considered Yellowstone's most powerful water feature. It is at its most impressive in spring, when

YPF Photo by Tom Porter

some 63,500gal of water cross its crest every second.

To best view the **Canyon and its Falls** – *see Drive below.*

Hayden Valley★★

This lush valley of meadow and marsh is the best place to observe **wildlife**. Hayden Valley is home to large herds of bison, plus moose and elk, and in spring is a good place to catch a glimpse of grizzly bears. Watching even a portion of the bison herd is as close as one can come to viewing life in the West before European settlement. Bears are often seen in spring and early summer, when they feed on newborn bison and elk calves. In summer, traffic backs up for miles when bison decide to cross the road. Turnouts, situated in key positions for viewing, may be occupied by a ranger with a spotting scope happily shared with visitors. You might see a bald eagle or even trumpeter swans in the valley. For a guided tour of the valley, *see Tours below.*

Mud Volcano

Heading south from Canyon Village toward Fishing Bridge, Grand Loop Road passes the Mud Volcano area.
Two of the area's most popular features include **Dragon's Mouth** and **Black Dragon's Caldron**. The turbulent hot spring and cavernous mouth give Dragon's Mouth Spring its name, though activity

has decreased considerably since 1994. Black Dragon's Caldron exploded onto the landscape in 1948, covering the surrounding forest with mud. Much of the hillside to the south and southwest of Mud Geyser steams and hisses due to a few combined mudpots.

DO

Check www.nps.gov/yell and www.YellowstoneNationalPark Lodges.com for current fees and schedules.

Summer

Children's Activities – The **Junior Ranger Programs** are designed for children ages 5-12, introducing them to the geology, history, and wildlife of Yellowstone. Stop in at the **Canyon Visitor Education Center** to find out about interactive programs that are geared to families with children of Junior Ranger age. Then meet a ranger in front of the Education Center for a 20-30 minute program.

Exhibits – The **Canyon Visitor Education Center** has interactive exhibits, animations, audio-visual productions and real-time scientific data on the Yellowstone volcano, its geysers and hot springs, and geologic history. Popular exhibits include a room-sized relief model of Yellowstone, a 9,000lb rotating Kugel globe highlighting volcanic hotspots and one of the world's largest lava lamps, illustrating how magma rises by heat convection.

Fishing – The **Yellowstone River, Cascade Lake** and **Grebe Lake** are popular fishing spots in the Canyon Area.

Hiking – Begin your hike by stopping at the **Canyon Visitor Education Center** for information. Trail conditions may change suddenly and unexpectedly. Bear activity, rain or snow storms, high water, and fires may temporarily close trails. There are numerous trails and viewpoints of the canyon falls from both **Canyon Rims** (the north rim and south rim); inquire at the Visitor Center for trail information.

• **Cascade Lake Trail**
Distance, round trip: 4.5 miles (7.2 km).
Difficulty: easy
Trailhead: Cascade Lake Picnic Area, 1.5 miles north of Canyon Jct. on the Tower-Canyon Road. This hike takes 3 hours through open meadows and over small creeks, offering wildlife and wildflowers in season. Most years, this trail remains very wet and muddy through July.

• **Grebe Lake Trail**
Distance, round trip: 6 miles (9.7 km).
Difficulty: moderate
Trailhead: 3.5 miles (5.6 km) west of Canyon Junction on the Norris-Canyon Road. This 3-4 hour hike has little vertical rise.

INSIDER TIP
OLD FAITHFUL VERSUS THE MUD VOLCANO

🐾 Just as mudpots look very different than hot springs, thermal areas at Yellowstone can have entirely different characters. Near Old Faithful in the Upper, Midway and Lower Geyser Basins, clear hot waters emerge in abundance, creating geysers, pools and springs that feed an estimated 400 gallons per second of thermal water to the Firehole River. Similar waters may exist beneath Mud Volcano, 23 miles away, but they certainly never make it to the surface. Instead, steam and gas rise from below, providing only a half gallon per second of thermal water to join the Yellowstone River. Nevertheless an estimated 500 gallons per second of gas, mostly carbon dioxide and hydrogen sulfide, diffuses out of the soils and bubbles through the mudpots at Mud Volcano. The result is not turquoise pools of clear alkaline waters, but smelly ponds of acid, murky water. What a difference!

Dr. Jake Lowenstern
US Geological Survey
Scientist-in-Charge,
Yellowstone Volcano
Observatory

This trail follows an old fire road through meadows and forest, some of which burned during the fires of 1988.

Horseback Riding – One-hour horseback rides are offered throughout the day. A two-hour ride is offered in the morning. Both leave from Canyon Lodge Corral, about a mile south of Canyon Lodge. Sign up in advance at the activities desk at Canyon Lodge or book by phone at 307-344-7311 or toll-free 1-866-439-7375.

Programs/Outings – Join a park ranger on the lower platform at **Artist Point** on South Rim Drive for a **15-minute talk** about the area's natural and human history. Learn about the ecology, geology, and history of the canyon while walking along the South Rim Trail with a ranger. Meet at **Uncle Tom's parking area** on South Rim Drive (road to Artist Point) for a **1.5 hour outing** involving an easy 1-mile walk. **Lupine Loop Walk** is a ranger-led 3-mile walk along the upper Grand Canyon of the Yellowstone River, then along an established trail through meadows and forest, before looping back to Uncle Tom's parking area on the South Rim. **Canyon Evening Programs** are 45-minute ranger-led illustrated programs about aspects of Yellowstone's natural or cultural history. Watch the local bulletin boards or inquire at the Canyon Visitor Education Center for program titles. Meet at the Canyon Campground **Amphitheater**.

Tours – The **Circle of Fire Tour** takes in Old Faithful, the Fountain Paint Pots and the Grand Canyon of the Yellowstone daily in summer. **Wildlife viewing tours** in the early evening hours are available daily in summer on the park's historic Yellow Buses with commentary along the way. Wildlife watching tours of **Hayden Valley** in the early morning are also available. Stop by the activities desk at Canyon Lodge or call 307-344-7311 (or toll-free 1-866-439-7375) for information and reservations for these tours.

Wildlife Viewing – *See Hayden Valley above.* Ospreys can sometimes be viewed in the Grand Canyon of the Yellowstone.

DRIVE
North Rim Drive
The 2.5mi North Rim Drive runs one-way from Canyon Village and provides several viewpoints. **Inspiration Point Drive** is a mile-long spur road off North Rim Drive that leads to several sights. Stop to see **Glacial Boulder**, a house-size granite boulder weighing about 500 tons that rests among pines alongside the road. It was extracted from the Beartooth Mountains by a glacier and dropped here nearly 80,000

years ago. A trailhead near the boulder leads to a view of **Silver Cord Cascade**, about a mile away. At the end of the road, **Inspiration Point**, a natural observation point, juts far out into the chasm, providing spectacular views of the canyon walls both upstream and down. **Grandview Point** affords another view of the canyon along with an opportunity to see osprey that nest above. Farther along, **Lookout Point** permits an unblocked view of the Lower Fall. From here, switchbacks and steps lead to **Red Rock Point**, a paved but very steep 1-mile trail that makes an even better place to see, hear and feel the falls crashing. Perhaps the most impressive view, however, can be found at **Brink of Lower Falls**, a taxing but rewarding steep descent of 600ft that takes you to the very edge where the water plunges over the rock wall.

South Rim Drive

Three miles south of Canyon Village, South Rim Drive heads east from Grand Loop Road and provides two popular viewpoints for the falls. **Uncle Tom's Trail** is a strenuous half-mile descent of some 330 metallic mesh steps down a rock face that provides access to a small viewing platform for what is considered one of the best views in Yellowstone. From here on sunny mornings, a brilliant rainbow is often seen in the spray of the falls. Just east

Crystal Falls is the outfall of Cascade Creek into the canyon. About one mile downstream, **Artist Point★★** is even more of a must see for an astounding view that has inspired painters, photographers, writers and explorers for hundreds of years. Although this photogenic scene is featured in most books about Yellowstone, standing here can inspire a full appreciation for the depth and colors of the canyon, beauty of the falls and power of the river below. The Yellowstone Park Foundation funded $1 million in restoration work, completed in 2008, to improve accessibility, repair stairs and platforms, and revegetate the landscape.

SHOP

(see Shopping p84)
Bookstore in Canyon Visitor Education Center
General Store
Gift Shop in Canyon Lodge
Outdoor Store.

EAT

(see Eating in the Park p87)
Canyon Lodge Dining Room
Canyon Cafeteria
Canyon Lodge Deli
Picnic Area – Cascade Lake Picnic Area is 1.5 miles north of Canyon Junction on Tower-Canyon Road.

STAY

(see Overnighting in the Park p90)
Canyon Lodge and Cabins
Canyon Campground

Like many of the park's natural wonders, Yellowstone Lake and its surroundings never cease to amaze. From the park's East Entrance, the road twists and turns through scenic country for 27 miles west to Fishing Bridge at the northern tip of the lake. The first 7 miles are particularly picturesque, with immense cliffs to the north and a heavily forested canyon to the south. Alongside this stretch of road during summer, colorful wildflowers abound and small waterfalls rush from above. A magnet for anglers, the deep lake not only proffers its prized cutthroat trout, but adds a bulwark of snow-dusted mountains as a majestic backdrop.

SEE

See map inside front cover.

East Entrance Road

Near **Sylvan Pass**, one of the highest points in the park at 8,541ft, the Absaroka Range can be readily seen. On the west side of the pass, descending through wooded areas and past placid Eleanor Lake and Sylvan Lake, a mile-long spur road leads to **Lake Butte Overlook**. This popular vantage point some 600ft above the lake is a favorite with photographers for its sublime view of the Teton Mountains, Mount Sheridan and Yellowstone Lake. Slightly northwest at Steamboat Point, **Steamboat Springs** is a thermal feature that puffs away at the lake's edge.

Yellowstone Lake

At 7,733ft altitude, the largest natural high-elevation lake in North America has 132sq miles of surface area, 141mi of shoreline and depths of nearly 400ft. Although the lake's surface is frozen half the year, water as hot as 252°F has been recorded in springs on the lake's floor. Recent studies have uncovered evidence of underwater geysers, hot springs and deep canyons: if the lake was somehow drained today, its thermal features would resemble those in other areas of the park. Osprey, bald eagles,

©Gwen Cannon/Michelin

white pelicans and cormorants can be readily seen in the skies above, while moose and grizzly bears can be found on the shore, particularly in the spring. Ringing its eastern shores, the bulky, snow-capped massif of the Absaroka Range adds a commanding presence.

Yellowstone River

The longest undammed river in the lower 48 states, the Yellowstone River runs north 671 miles. It originates in the southeast, flows into Yellowstone Lake, exiting at Fishing Bridge and meandering through the Grand Canyon of the Yellowstone before continuing to its confluence with the Missouri River.

Fishing Bridge Museum and Visitor Center

Located one mile off Grand Loop Road on East Entrance Road, this visitor center was built in 1931. A National Historic Landmark, it is famed for its distinctive native rock-and-log construction, known as

NPS Photo by Jim Peaco

INSIDER TIP
FISHING BRIDGE

🐾 Here's a little history to "bridge" yesterday with today. Initially a ferry was planned to span the Yellowstone River north and east of Yellowstone Lake, but a simple wooden bridge with a slightly arched belly (for rowboat access) was built instead. It was completed in 1902 and was appropriately called "Fishing Bridge" by 1914. This fishing was phenomenal, and a typical scene found anglers elbow to elbow filling coolers with native cutthroat trout. Five years later the bridge was rebuilt. The current bridge, built in 1937, assumed the old name and accommodated the increased traffic of automobiles, pedestrians, and anglers. People joke today that it should be called No Fishing Bridge to reflect the fact that fishing was stopped from the bridge and nearby waters to protect cutthroat trout spawning grounds in 1973. Don't be tempted to fish from Fishing Bridge!

Karen Reinhart
Former Yellowstone Park Ranger Interpreter
Author, Old Faithful Inn: Crown Jewel of National Park Lodges **and** Yellowstone's Rebirth by Fire: Rising from the Ashes of the 1988 Fires

Left to right: Yellowstone Lake, Yellowstone River

"parkitecture," which became a prototype for park buildings around the country. It has an on-site bookstore and a number of amusing wildlife **exhibits.** *See Exhibits below.*

Fishing Bridge

Nearby, at the point where the Yellowstone River flows north from Yellowstone Lake, this bridge extends over the neck of the river where trout come to spawn beginning in June. The original 1902-bridge was replaced in 1937 and remained a popular casting point for decades. In 1973 fishing was banned from the bridge, but it remains a destination for fish watching.

Lake Village

Overlooking the lake from its northwest shore, **Lake Yellowstone Hotel★** dominates the village. The stately, three-story hotel was built in 1891 and retains a few of its original features (*free tours of the hotel; see Tours below*). Yellow clapboard with white trim; the exterior received its first major facelift in 1903 when architect Robert Reamer added ionic columns and 15 false balconies. No hotel has stood in any national park longer than Lake Yellowstone Hotel (*see Overnighting in the Park*).

Bridge Bay

A few miles south of Fishing Bridge and Lake Village,

Bridge Bay is home to a marina, an outdoor store and large campground. There's also the Bridge Bay Ranger Station and an amphitheater for park programs.

Natural Bridge

This cliff of rhyolite lava was sculpted into an overpass by Bridge Creek, which runs underneath. At a height of about 50ft, the graceful arch is located just south of Bridge Bay, an easy one-mile journey by bike path or trail. Travel across the 30ft overpass, however, is prohibited.

DO

Check www.nps.gov/yell and www.YellowstoneNationalPark Lodges.com for current fees and schedules.

Summer

Biking – For details, access www.nps.gov/yell/planyourvisit/bicycling.htm. Inquire at the visitor center about trail closures before biking these trails.

Cycling is permitted on the following routes (for a **map of biking routes** in the park, visit www.nps.gov/yell/planyourvisit):

Natural Bridge Service Road near Bridge Bay; it's the old roadbed near the lakeshore between Lake Yellowstone Hotel and the juncture of the roadbed and the main road south of Lake Junction (1 mile). The bicycle trail to the bridge begins just south of Bridge Bay marina, off the main road.

The old roadbed along the lakeshore between **Lake Yellowstone Hotel and Grand Loop Road** (1 mile).

Boating – **Boating** is allowed on most of Yellowstone Lake. A permit is required for all motorized and non-motorized vessels (including float tubes) and must be obtained in person from the **Bridge Bay Ranger Station** or other park office. A personal flotation device is required for each person boating. Be forewarned that lake waters can rapidly change from still to very choppy. Boating-related fatalities on the lake have resulted from hypothermia. Outboards and rowboats may be rented from Xanterra Parks and Resorts at **Bridge Bay Marina**; guided fishing boats may be reserved in advance by calling (307) 344-7311 or 866-439-7375. See boating regulations and fees online at www.nps.gov/yell/planyourvisit/boating.htm.

For a narrated **boat tour**, *see Tours below.*

Children's Activities – **Family Campfire** programs lasting 45 minutes are available in summer especially for families with young children. **Junior Ranger** programs are also available. Inquire about both programs at Fishing Bridge Visitor Center or look on local bulletin boards for the day's subject. Meet at Bridge Bay Campground Amphitheater.

Exhibits – The **Fishing Bridge Museum and Visitor Center** is located one mile off Grand Loop Road on the East Entrance Road. Historic bird specimens by Carl Russell were installed in 1931 to provide a good overview of the birds of Yellowstone. Other taxidermied animals are displayed here as well as river otters. The East Wing houses a bookstore.

Left to right: *Bridge Bay Marina, Picnic along the shore*

NPS Photo

NPS Photo by William S. Keller

Fishing – Home to the largest concentration of cutthroat trout in America, the lake is a haven for fishermen. However, it can be temperamental for boaters, with rapidly changing conditions from still waters to considerably choppy. Many of the lake's boat-related fatalities result from hypothermia. For guided charters/trips, see authorized outfitters at www.nps.gov/yell/planyourvisit/fishbsn.htm.

Bridge Creek is another favored fishing hole. Note that you cannot fish from Fishing Bridge. Until 1973 this was a very popular fishing location since the bridge crossed the Yellowstone River above a cutthroat trout spawning area. It is now a popular place to observe fish. Yellowstone cutthroat trout are currently imperiled due to the illegal introduction of non-native lake trout. This invasive species is predatory, with each lake trout consuming at least 41 cutthroat trout each year. The result affects the entire food chain since lake trout swim too deep in the lake to be a food source for bears, raptors and other wildlife.

Hiking – There are several hiking trails in the Lake Area. Natural Bridge Trail is closed from late spring to early summer due to bears feeding on spawning trout in Bridge Creek. Before hiking, inquire at the visitor center about trail closures and weather conditions.

• **Natural Bridge Trail**
Distance, round trip: 3 miles (5 km).
Difficulty: easy
Trailhead: Bridge Bay Marina parking lot, near the campground entrance road. The trail meanders through the forest for 1.2 mile (0.8 km). It then joins the road and continues to the right (west) for 1 mile (1.5 km) before reaching the Natural Bridge. The short but steep switchback trail to the top of the bridge starts in front of the interpretive exhibit. To protect this fragile resource, the top of the bridge is closed to hiking.

NPS Photo by Jim Peaco

However, good views may be attained next to the bridge.

• Storm Point Trail
Distance, round trip: 2 miles (3 km) loop.
Difficulty: easy
Trailhead: Pullout at Indian Pond, 3 miles (5 km) east of Fishing Bridge Visitor Center. This trail begins in open meadows overlooking **Indian Pond** and Yellowstone Lake. The trail passes the pond before turning right (west) into the forest. Continuing through the trees, it comes out to windswept **Storm Point**. The rocky area near the point is home to a large colony of yellow-bellied marmots. Following the shoreline to the west, the trail eventually loops through the lodgepole pine forest and returns to Indian Pond.

Programs/Outings –
Ranger-led 2hr, 2.3 mile, easy hike. Meet at the Storm Point Trailhead, 3 miles east of Fishing Bridge. The moderately strenuous, 2hr **Mud Volcano Ramble** explores intriguing

NPS Photo

INSIDER TIP
YELLOWSTONE LAKE'S NORTHSIDE

🐾 A pleasant stroll is found east of Fishing Bridge, where evidence abounds for rare but strong *hydrothermal* or *steam* explosions. Park at the Indian Pond trailhead and head out towards Yellowstone Lake. The pond, a common place to see colorful grebes and goldeneyes, was formed by a steam explosion some 2,900 years ago. Continue to Storm Point and you'll see young thermal features and rock outcroppings from earlier explosions. Look to the east and observe Mary Bay, formed 13,000 years ago by the world's largest known steam explosion. The walls of this 2-mile-diameter bay are made of boulders ejected during the formative eruptions. As you gaze, you'll be standing close to the site where the USGS Hayden Expedition camped on August 20, 1871, a place they called "Earthquake Camp" for the constant tremors they felt.

Dr. Jake Lowenstern
US Geological Survey
Scientist-in-Charge,
Yellowstone Volcano
Observatory

Left to right: *Thundershowers over Yellowstone Lake, Yellowstone Lake shoreline* mudpots and hot springs. Meet at the Mud Volcano parking area for this hike.

From a picturesque spot along the Yellowstone River, trace Fishing Bridge area history and one of the most important cogs in the motor of the Yellowstone ecosystem: the polka-dotted cutthroat trout. Meet on the west side of the Fishing Bridge for a 20-minute program.

In summer, illustrated, ranger-led **evening programs** last 45-minutes. Inquire at Fishing Bridge Visitor Center or check local bulletin boards for each night's subject. Meet at Fishing Bridge Visitor Center Amphitheater. Evening programs are also held at Bridge Bay Campground Amphitheater.

Tours – Scenicruises on Yellowstone Lake are available in summer. The 1hr narrated boat tours, sometimes accompanied by a park ranger, offer views of the Absaroka Range, historic Lake Yellowstone Hotel, and the surrounding lodgepole pine forest. Reservations required in advance through Xanterra Parks & Resorts. Call 307-344-7311 or stop by the **Bridge Bay Marina**. Take an early morning **Photo Safari** with a photographer-guide who knows the ideal spots for photo shoots. A muffin, coffee and juice will be provided. Daily departures from Lake Yellowstone Hotel in summer for experienced and novice shutterbugs.

Free **Lake Yellowstone Hotel Tour** with an interpretive guide who revisits the history, the hardships, and oddities of Yellowstone's oldest hotel; daily from the Lake Hotel Lobby. Lake Butte Sunset Tours offer breathtaking views of Yellowstone Lake from the Lake Butte Overlook. Daily departures in summer from the Lake Hotel and Fishing Bridge RV Park. Inquire for the above tours at the Lake Hotel or call 307-344-7311 (or toll-free 1-866-439-7375) for information, fees and reservations.

Wildlife Viewing – The skies above **Yellowstone Lake** are routinely abuzz with osprey, bald eagles, white pelicans and cormorants; common loons frequent its waters and along the shore, moose and grizzly bears amble, especially in springtime.

DRIVE
Gull Point Drive

Less than a mile south of Fishing Bridge, Gull Point Drive, a side road off Grand Loop Road, hugs the shoreline of Yellowstone Lake, permitting exquisite views of the lake's deep-blue waters and the Absaroka mountains.

Amid Engelmann spruce and subalpine fir, amblers can stroll the lakeshore, fish the lake, and enjoy a picnic at Gull Point Picnic Area, which has plenty of picnic tables and a public

toilet. East of the picnic area, Stevenson Island sits in the lake.

SHOP
(*see Shopping p84*)
Bookstore in Fishing Bridge Visitor Center
General Store at Fishing Bridge
Lake Yellowstone Hotel Gift Shop
Lake Lodge Gift Shop
Outdoor Store at Bridge Bay.

EAT
(*see Eating in the Park p87*)
Lake Yellowstone Hotel Dining Room
Lake Yellowstone Hotel Deli
Lake Lodge Cafeteria
Picnic Areas – Picnic areas around the lake: (east to west and then south) Sedge Bay, Steamboat Point, Fishing Bridge, Lake Village, Bridge Bay, Gull Point, Sand Point and Spruce/Fir Exhibit.

STAY
(*see Overnighting in the Park p90*)
Lake Yellowstone Hotel and Cabins
Lake Lodge Cabins
Campgrounds – The large campground at **Bridge Bay** is located near Yellowstone Lake and adjacent to Bridge Bay Marina.
Fishing Bridge RV Park sits near Fishing Bridge Junction.

Top to bottom: *Yellowstone Lake, Bald eagle in nest, Fishing Bridge RV Park*

Anchoring the park's southern end, Grant Village is the first way station to greet visitors who enter the park via the South Entrance. Just north, the West Thumb Geyser Basin is perhaps the most beautifully situated thermal area in Yellowstone. Early explorers described the shape of Yellowstone Lake as a human hand with fingers extending southward. Its "thumb," on the west end of the lake, is actually a small collapsed caldera created during an explosion about 160,000 years ago within the larger Yellowstone caldera. Historically, visitors to Yellowstone traditionally entered this region from the Old Faithful area by stagecoach, crossing Craig Pass (8,262ft) and the Continental Divide along the 17-mile journey east to West Thumb Junction.

SEE
See map inside front cover.

South Entrance Road
The South Entrance Road runs about 22 miles up to the West Thumb junction, where it meets Grand Loop Road. The road first passes a turnoff for **Moose Falls**, a delightful 30ft waterfall on Crawfish Creek, accessible by a short hike from the road. **Lewis Canyon** enters sight from this point on, its dramatic scenery scarred by the 1988 fires. A pleasant view of **Lewis Falls**, which plunges about 30ft, can be seen farther along. The road then continues northward along the edge of Lewis Lake, named for explorer **Meriwether Lewis**, who missed Yellowstone by about 50 miles during the famed 1804 Lewis and Clark Expedition. To the east, **Mount Sheridan** (10,308ft), the highest peak of the Red Mountains, towers in the distance.

Grant Village
Named in honor of President Ulysses S. Grant, who signed legislation that created Yellowstone in 1872, this full-service park community has a ranger station, store, motel-type lodgings (*see Stay below*), campground, picnic area, and boat launch, among other amenities. The **Grant**

Forest Fires
The 1988 fires affected 793,880 acres or 36 percent of Yellowstone National Park. Five fires burned into the park that year from adjacent public lands. The largest, the North Fork Fire, started from a discarded cigarette, which burned more than 410,000 acres.

©Johnny Brian/age fotostock

Village Visitor Center is located here, along the shore of the West Thumb of Yellowstone Lake, one mile off the main park road at Grant Village Junction. It features a small exhibit depicting fire's role in the Yellowstone ecosystem (*see Exhibits below*). Because it is situated among a forest of lodgepole pines, this area was greatly impacted by the 1988 fires in the park.

West Thumb Geyser Basin★

Just east of West Thumb Junction, located along the lake's shore, this dense cluster of colorful hot springs, pools, mudpots, fumaroles and lakeshore geysers is considered the most scenic geyser basin in the park. Because of the lower amount of sulfur emitted in this area, its rotten egg smell is not as strong as elsewhere in the park. The approximately half-mile boardwalk winds through the shoreline of thermal features including the cobalt-blue **Abyss Pool★**, one of the park's deepest pools at about 50ft,

INSIDER TIP
GEYSERS AND POOLS

🐾 You can learn about a pool's behavior simply by looking at its surroundings. Pools with smooth, flat overhanging edges, often with scalloped margins, testify to a "quiet lifestyle" with relatively constant water levels. In contrast, spiny or warty silica deposits reveal the splashes and gurgles from a nearby active geyser. If you can look around and see boulders that surround the pool, you may be looking at the remains of a powerful rock-hurling steam explosion that gave the pool its origins. Or if the water in the pool is dark and murky, it's filled with low-temperature algae and hasn't been active in years.

Dr. Jake Lowenstern
US Geological Survey
Scientist-in-Charge,
Yellowstone Volcano
Observatory

Left to right: *Fishing Cone Geyser, Abyss Pool*

©Alessandra Sarti/age fotostock

which appears to be bottomless. It continues on to **Black Pool**, once darker in color, but today, as it cools, it often appears blue or green. The basin's most popular attraction is **Fishing Cone Geyser★**, a hot spring situated on the shore that once served as a source of heat for cooking fish on the hook. "Boiling trout" here became a tradition for early visitors to the park. Today, however, fishing at or near the cone is prohibited. South of Fishing Cone, **Lakeshore Geyser** is often covered by cold lake water. Farther inland, mudpots and fumaroles remain active, bubbling and steaming along the shore, which is particularly scenic at sunrise.

Shoshone Lake

Named for the Shoshone Indians who frequented its banks, Shoshone Lake is the second largest lake in Yellowstone. It is the source of the **Lewis River**, which flows to the Pacific

Below: *Lewis River*

©Luis Castañeda/age fotostock

Ocean via the Snake River system. There is no road access to the lake. The **Shoshone Geyser Basin** near the lake's far western shore is the park's largest backcountry thermal area, containing about 100 thermal features. There is no boardwalk here, so caution is advised.

Riddle Lake

Located three miles south of the West Thumb bay of Yellowstone Lake, this "mythical lake" was believed by early explorers to flow east and west to two oceans. The riddle was solved when it was confirmed that the lake's outlet, consequently named Solution Creek, flows to Yellowstone Lake. The lake waters are covered with lily pads and backdropped to the south by the Red Mountains, a small range completely contained within the boundaries of the park.

Heart Lake

Sitting at the base of Mount Sheridan, Heart Lake is a popular destination for backcountry overnight trips. **Heart Lake Geyser Basin**, a highlight of the area, is located along Witch Creek on the lake's western shore. Like most of this area's thermal features, the two primary attractions, Rustic Geyser and Columbia Pool, are in nearly pristine condition. Towering in the west are the **Red Mountains**.

Cascade Corner

To the far west of South Entrance Road, tucked away in the rugged southwest corner of the park, this concentrated area of waterfalls, pools and cascades cannot be accessed by any road that connects in the park. Also known as the Belcher Area, it is a waterfall-lover's paradise and includes **Union Falls** (260ft), the second highest falls in the park aside from the Lower Falls of the Grand Canyon. Union Falls is widely known as one of the most spectacular waterfalls in Yellowstone: along with cascade-like ribbons of water, twin streams of frothy water gush over the sheer face of the rock into a pool below.

DO

Check www.nps.gov/yell and www.YellowstoneNationalPark Lodges.com for current fees and schedules.

Summer

Boating – Boating is allowed on **Lewis Lake**. Only non-motorized boating (canoes, kayaks) is allowed on most other lakes and one river: the **Lewis Channel** between Lewis Lake and Shoshone Lake. Permits can be obtained from the visitor center.

Exhibits – Grant Village Visitor Center features an exhibit about fire's role in Yellowstone, using the fires of 1988 as the example. A fire movie is shown on a regular

INSIDER TIP
FISHING'S EARLY AND LATE SEASONS AND SNOWMELT

🐾 The first river to be cleared of snowmelt is the **Firehole River**, which is often the only river in fishable condition when the park opens to fishing the Saturday of Memorial Day weekend. The Firehole usually offers up great dry-fly fishing during afternoon mayfly and caddis hatches and continues to do so until the end of June. By the 4th of July nearly all of Yellowstone rivers will run clear of snowmelt.

🐾 In Yellowstone's late season, from September to early November, only a few hatches remain to bring trout to the surface. Huge Fall Green Drakes will come off now on the Lamar River and Slough and Soda Butte Creeks as will tiny mayflies like the Blue-Winged Olives and midges. The Madison and Firehole Rivers produce excellent dry-fly fishing in late season during caddis, midge and mayfly emergences. October is the best month to visit if you want to catch the large migrating fish in the Madison and Lewis Rivers.

Craig Mathews
Nationally recognized fly-fishing guide, Blue Ribbon Flies, West Yellowstone

schedule here throughout the summer. West Thumb Information Station, which serves as a warming hut in winter, has interpretive exhibits on Yellowstone's history and a variety of winter topics.

Fishing – Unreachable by road, **Shoshone Lake** has lake trout, brown trout, and Utah chubs. No motorboats are allowed on the lake. **Lewis Lake's** shoreline and **Aster Creek** near Lewis Falls are especially suitable for novice and young anglers.

Hiking – Several trails, including Lake Overlook Trail, Duck Lake Trail and Riddle Lake Trail, provide opportunities to examine the various stages of lodgepole pine forest succession and development as well as fire ecology. The West Thumb Geyser Basin Trail follows a boardwalk to the basin.

• West Thumb Geyser Basin Trail
Distance, round trip: 3/8 miles (.6 km).
Difficulty: easy (boardwalk trail with slight grade as trail descends to and climbs up from the lakeshore)
Trailhead: West Thumb Geyser Basin, 1/4 mile east of West Thumb Junction. Stroll through a geyser basin of colorful hot springs and dormant lakeshore geysers situated on the scenic shores of Yellowstone Lake.

Trails; and boardwalks are handicapped-accessible, with assistance.

• Lake Overlook Trail
Distance, round trip: 2 miles (3 km).
Difficulty: moderate; mostly level terrain with a moderately strenuous 400-foot elevation gain near the overlook.
Trailhead: Trailhead sign at entrance to West Thumb Geyser Basin parking area. Hike to a high mountain meadow for a commanding view of the West Thumb of Yellowstone Lake and the Absaroka Mountains.

Programs/Outings – You can obtain details and times from the visitor center for the following programs:
Prospective **Junior Rangers** may participate in 20-minute interactive programs designed just for them. Meet on the Grant Visitor Center back porch.
Fire Walk programs – Without fire, Yellowstone would not be the park we see today. Join a ranger-led 30-minute tour to examine the scene of a recent burn. Meet at the long pullout with the vault toilet 6.8 miles (10.9 km) north of West Thumb Junction.
Evening programs of 30 minutes' duration about Yellowstone's diverse geology, history, or wildlife are held at the Grant Village Amphitheater.

DRIVE
West Thumb Bay Shore
Leave West Thumb basin area and drive north on **Grand Loop Road**, passing Duck Lake on your left. The road parallels the bay's shoreline along the northwest section of the bay. The drive permits grand views of the bay of the West Thumb of Yellowstone Lake and the Absaroka Range in the distance. You'll pass the turnoff for Hard Road to Travel Picnic Area on the left. Continue to Fisherman's Access Picnic Area (with picnic tables and restroom) to enjoy a packed lunch before returning to West Thumb.

SHOP
(see Shopping p84)
Bookstores at West Thumb Information Station and Grant Village Visitor Center
Grant Village Gift Shop (in the registration building)
General Store.

EAT
(see Eating in the Park p87)
Grant Village Dining Room
Grant Village Lake House Restaurant
Picnic Areas – Near the South Entrance, **Snake River Picnic Area**. Just south of Lewis Lake is the **Lewis Lake Picnic Area**. **Grant Village** has a picnic area, as does **West Thumb**.

STAY
(see Overnighting in the Park p90)
Grant Village motel lodgings
Grant Village Campground

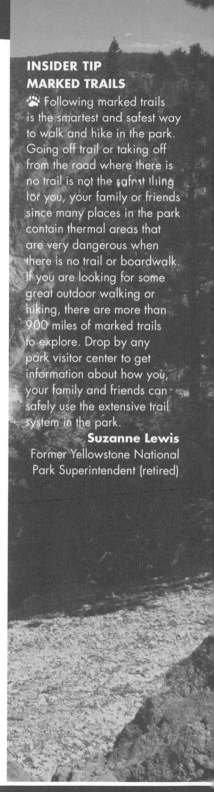

INSIDER TIP
MARKED TRAILS
Following marked trails is the smartest and safest way to walk and hike in the park. Going off trail or taking off from the road where there is no trail is not the safest thing for you, your family or friends since many places in the park contain thermal areas that are very dangerous when there is no trail or boardwalk. If you are looking for some great outdoor walking or hiking, there are more than 900 miles of marked trails to explore. Drop by any park visitor center to get information about how you, your family and friends can safely use the extensive trail system in the park.
Suzanne Lewis
Former Yellowstone National Park Superintendent (retired)

Wildlife Viewing and Photography
Safe Viewing of Animals

The number one attraction at Yellowstone is wildlife viewing. The number one safety issue is getting too close to the wildlife for viewing and photography. Visitors want their photo taken with wildlife in the background, yet this arrangement puts you, your family or friends at grave risk. Why? because more than likely you will turn your back to the animals and the person taking the photo will be looking through the lens or at the screen on a smart device and will not be paying attention to what the wildlife may be doing.

Here is what you can do to ensure your safety and take home some great photos. First, obey all the park regulations as to how far away you must keep from all wildlife at all times (at least 100 yards away from wolves and bears, and at least 25 yards from all other wildlife); second, stand to the side and never with your back to the animals; and third, use all the zoom power you have to get the animals in the background. These simple steps will ensure that you get good photos SAFELY.

Suzanne Lewis
Former Yellowstone National Park Superintendent (retired)

Photographing Wildlife

Magnificent photographs are available every day here, if we go out to find them. The best time to observe wildlife is early in the morning from just before sunrise until mid-morning and late in the evening. The best wildlife photographs illustrate part of a creature's life in its natural home. Wildlife here is wild and wants to go about its daily life doing what it wants to do. Do not approach any animal, whistle or shout at it.

YPF Photo by Tom Porter

The best wildlife photographs are those in which we can see the normal, natural behavior of the animals, and get a sense of what their life is like.

Tom Murphy
Author and natural history photographer

Park Photography

For 25 years I hiked the backcountry with a 60-pound pack filled with camera gear. I felt that no photo was good enough unless shot far from the park road. Yet most of my best sequences were taken near the road. In the backcountry, animals are not expecting you, and often run away. Furthermore, it is not safe to film grizzlies at less than 100 yards, even if they tolerate your presence.

Animals are present roadside because they have come there by choice—and they accept human presence. Dangerous animals like grizzly bears and bison may be filmed at reasonable range without posing a threat. Driving the road allows the photographer to investigate far more territory than by foot, and more importantly, thousands of "game spotters" (park visitors) will locate animals for you: just look for the scopes and telephoto lenses.

My recommendation for getting intimate photos of wild animals is to stay near the road. By all means hike the backcountry, but save weight by leaving your camera gear behind.

Bob Landis
Emmy-award-winning filmmaker specializing in Yellowstone wildlife films

Opposite: *Black bear*
Below: *Wolf with pups*

NPS Photo

SHOPPING IN THE PARK

Yellowstone National Park offers visitors a surprisingly broad shopping experience, one that meets practical needs as well as satisfying a desire to bring home memories of a rewarding stay. Recreational gear, souvenirs and crafts, books, apparel, jewelry, ceramic ware, stuffed animals, totes, food and more can be found in the park bookstores, gift shops and general stores. There are even two ski shops open in the winter season that rent equipment as well as sell gear and clothing.

Bookstores

Bookstores in the park visitor centers are run by the **Yellowstone Association**, the park's official education partner. A wide range of books is available on general and park-related topics such as wildlife, photography, weather, ecology, geology, history, plants and recreation. Park guidebooks and children's books are also on hand. Other items for sale include road and hiking **maps** and videos of Yellowstone. Proceeds from store purchases and memberships are donated to Yellowstone National Park to support research and education. Bookstores follow visitor center hours and are generally **open late-May–early Oct**, unless otherwise noted below. Bookstores in Mammoth, Old Faithful, Gardiner, and Bozeman are also open in winter season.

- Albright Visitor Center Bookstore, Mammoth Area (open year-round)
- Canyon Visitor Education Center Bookstore
- Fishing Bridge Visitor Center Bookstore
- Yellowstone Association Headquarters in Gardiner, MT (open year-round)
- Gallatin Field Airport in Bozeman, MT (open year-round)
- Grant Visitor Center Bookstore

Left to right: *Yellowstone Association Bookstore, Yellowstone General Store*

Yellowstone Association photo by Pam Cahill

- Madison Information Station Bookstore
- Norris Geyser Basin Museum Bookstore
- Old Faithful Visitor Education Center Bookstore (closed early Nov–mid-Dec and mid-Mar–mid-Apr)
- West Thumb Information Station Bookstore

General Stores

Yellowstone General Stores in the park are operated by concessioner **Delaware North Companies Parks and Resorts at Yellowstone**. The stores sell park-emblazoned apparel, groceries, camping and fishing gear, supplies, housewares and collectibles. Yellowstone blankets, stationery, journals and stuffed animals are among items that can serve as mementos. They also carry an excellent selection of Yellowstone-branded Pendleton blankets and other merchandise, especially at the Fishing Bridge Store. Some stores include fountain food service on the premises (*see Restaurants below*).

Stores are open mid- or late-May to late Sept or early Oct, except Mammoth, which is open in winter and summer seasons.

- Canyon Village General Store
- Fishing Bridge General Store
- Grant Village General Store
- Grant Village Mini Store
- Lake Village General Store
- Mammoth General Store
- Old Faithful Lower General Store
- Old Faithful Upper General Store
- Tower General Store
- Roosevelt General Store

Gift Shops

Park gift shops are operated by lodging and dining concessioner **Xanterra Parks & Resorts**. These shops stock gifts, gourmet foods, apparel, jewelry, souvenirs, tote bags, publications, stationery and a variety of other merchandise. Most shops are open mid-May to early Oct. The Bear Den at Old Faithful Snow Lodge is open mid-Apr until early Nov.

Canyon Lodge Gift Shop sells various Canyon-themed

Yellowstone General Stores

Green Products
When browsing in Xanterra gift shops, look for the "Sustain the Earth" logo, which designates sustainable products. Be sure to use a reusable shopping bag or buy a tote bag. Park restaurants also offer a variety of "green" choices such as Marine Stewardship Council certified salmon and fair trade organic coffee.

items as well as Yellowstone-emblazoned and outdoor-themed clothing.

Grant Village Gift Shop
(in the Grant Village registration building) offers items and supplies that are customized to this area of the park, along with other souvenirs, apparel and travel products.

Lake Lodge Gift Shop
carries note cards, souvenirs, housewares, clothing, and supplies, both park-emblazoned or nature-themed.

Lake Yellowstone Hotel Gift Shop
boasts the largest selection of apparel in the park, as well as regional merchandise.

For Future Generations: Yellowstone Gifts,
in Mammoth Hot Springs Hotel, embodies a cutting edge concept in retail stores. The shop focuses on environmentally friendly products, interpretive messaging about climate change and guest education on sustainability initiatives in Yellowstone.

Old Faithful Inn Gift Shop
markets memorable gifts, from keepsakes to fine apparel. Its specialty is a wide selection of pottery with both traditional and Native-American designs.

Old Faithful Lodge Gift Shop
carries themed items reminiscent of the park experience and a large selection of ceramics.

Roosevelt Lodge Gift Shop
reflects the spirit of the Old West. Here you'll find a variety of Western memorabilia, jewelry and Native American crafts.

Outdoor Stores
These stores are operated by Yellowstone General Stores. They carry recreational gear, souvenirs, and snacks. They also serve some grab-and-go food items.
- **Bridge Bay Outdoor Store** (late-May to early Sept)
- **Yellowstone Adventures Store**, located next to Canyon Visitor Education Center (mid-Apr through the park's closing)

Ski Shops
Xanterra Parks & Resorts' **Bear Den** Ski Shops (mid-Dec to early Mar) are located in Old Faithful Snow Lodge and Mammoth Hotel. They stock winter sports apparel and gear, rent skis and snowshoes and arrange instruction. Expert staff can help you plan your day on the trails and provide information on snow conditions, ski shuttles, and tours in the park.

EATING IN THE PARK

Xanterra Parks & Resorts offers visitors a variety of in-park dining options. There are sit-down restaurants in every village. Cafeterias set out fresh salads, sandwiches and pastas. Full-service dining rooms prepare a selection of appetizers, entrées and desserts. Delis and snack shops cater to on-the-go customers with take-out foods. Roosevelt Lodge arranges popular Old West Dinner Cookouts. While dress is always casual, restaurant menus and atmospheres range from casual to upscale.

Cafeterias
Canyon Lodge Cafeteria features themed stations with both hot and cold items at lunch and dinner (early Jun to early Sept).

Lake Lodge Cafeteria offers salads and take-out foods, daily specials and a view of Yellowstone Lake. Breakfast, lunch and dinner are served (mid-Jun to early Oct).

Old Faithful Lodge Cafeteria has serving stations with meats, pastas, salads, sandwiches and other items at lunch and dinner (mid-May to late-Sept).

Delis and Snack Shops
Canyon Lodge Deli is the place for take-out sandwiches, salads, chips, drinks and ice cream (early Jun to late-Sept).

Lake Hotel Deli gives customers to-go options like sandwiches, soups and other fare (late May to late-Sept).

Old Faithful Inn's **Bear Paw Deli** sells specialty sandwiches, salads, ice cream and other take-out items (early May to early Oct).

Old Faithful Lodge Cafeteria's Bake Shop bakes cinnamon rolls, muffins, cookies, and bread for deli sandwiches (mid-May to late-Sept).

Restaurants
Canyon Lodge Dining Room has a breakfast buffet and menu; à la carte lunches of wraps, burgers and grilled sandwiches; and dinner choices like roasted prime rib (early Jun to late Sept).

Grant Village Dining Room prepares breakfast, lunch and dinner. Dinner brings meat, pasta and vegetarian choices (late-May to early Oct).

Grant Village Lake House Restaurant serves pub-style food and microbrews in a casual setting at dinnertime. Breakfast is buffet style (mid-Jun to late Sept). No lunch is served.

Lake Yellowstone Hotel Dining Room offers a breakfast buffet and menu; sandwiches, soups and salads at lunch; and game, seafood and vegetarian dishes at dinner. Dinner reservations required (late-May to late-Sept).

Mammoth Hot Springs Hotel Dining Room serves three meals a day. At dinner, small plate items and entrées like seafood, prime rib and pasta are crowd-pleasers (mid-May to mid-Oct and late-Dec to early Mar).

The Obsidian Restaurant at Old Faithful Snow Lodge offers inspired preparations of beef, pasta, fish and vegetarian dishes. For breakfast, there's a buffet or an à la carte menu (early May to late-Oct and late-Dec to early Mar).

Old Faithful Inn Dining Room is a spacious log dining hall awash in rustic elegance. Open for breakfast, lunch and dinner, this restaurant is one of the more popular. In addition to a full menu, buffets are available at all meals. Dinner reservations are required (early May to early Oct).

Roosevelt Lodge Dining Room features dining with a cowboy flare. Barbeque ribs

and signature Roosevelt Baked Beans are long-time favorites, while traditional fare is available at breakfast (mid-Jun to early Sept).

Yellowstone General Stores' fountains vary from 1950s-diner-inspired counter service at **Canyon Village** to casual cafeterias and ice cream parlors. Or skip the traditional sit-down restaurant experience and stock up on groceries, snacks, sandwiches and other light fare in the store. If you choose to sit down, the following General Stores provide seating for food-service customers.
- Canyon Village General Store
- Fishing Bridge General Store
- Grant Village General Store
- Lake Village General Store
- Tower-Roosevelt General Store

Grills

Mammoth's **Terrace Grill** prepares quick orders and take-out food at breakfast, lunch and dinner (late-Apr to mid-Oct).

Old Faithful Snow Lodge Geyser Grill offers burgers, hot and cold sandwiches, salads, beverages and desserts (mid-Apr to early Nov and late-Dec to early Mar).

Lounges

Most park lodges have lounges in which to relax and enjoy a drink after sightseeing, whether or not you're staying overnight in the lodge itself. Signature beverages as well as regional

Box Lunches

Park lodges and inns will prepare a carry-out lunch for visitors upon request (sandwich plus raisins, chips, cookies and bottled water). Place your order **the night before** at any dining room and pick it up at breakfast. You do not need to be an overnight guest at the hotel to order a lunch. Pre-made sandwiches and salads are also available at cafeterias, delis and snack shops at hotels and lodges around the park.

microbrews are available at most lounges.

- Bear Pit Lounge in the Old Faithful Inn
- Canyon Lodge Lounge
- Firehole Lounge in Old Faithful Snow Lodge
- Seven Stool Lounge at Grant Village
- Reamer Lounge and Sun Room at Lake Hotel
- Lake Lodge Lounge
- Mammoth Hot Springs Hotel Lounge
- Roosevelt Lodge Lobby Bar

Picnic Areas

The park's 50 roadside picnic areas usually have toilets but no drinking water (Madison has drinking water). You can use camping stoves and self-contained charcoal grills at any picnic area. Fires are permitted only in fire grates. Because of bears, never leave food outside your vehicle or around your picnic table or campsite—not even inside a cooler—when you are away or asleep. Some picnic areas have wheelchair-accessible restrooms.For a list of picnic areas, visit www.nps.gov/yell.

Top to bottom: *Grant Village Restaurant, Obsidian Restaurant, Canyon Village 1950s-diner-inspired fountain, Old Faithful Lodge Cafeteria*

OVERNIGHTING IN THE PARK

To reflect the natural surroundings, Yellowstone's lodgings have no TVs (except Mammoth Hotel suites), radios or air conditioning (but fans are provided). Internet service is available for a fee at the Old Faithful Snow Lodge and the Mammoth Hotel Dining Room Lounge. Most guest rooms have telephones, but cabins do not. Wheelchair-accessible rooms are available on a limited basis. All park accommodations are non-smoking. For reservations, access www.YellowstoneNationalParkLodges.com or call toll-free 866-GEYSERLAND (866-439-7375) or 307-344-7311. For the best selection of lodging location and room type, it is recommended that you reserve a minimum of six months in advance.

Cabins

Canyon Lodge Cabins (early Jun to late-Sept) are Western motel-style units of 4 or 6 with private bath and 2 queen beds. Frontier cabins are modest motel-style units of 4 or 8 with private baths with shower, toilet and sink.

Lake Lodge (early Jun to early Oct) offers Western motel-style cabins in 4 or 6 units with 2 queen beds and private baths with shower or tub; Frontier

Left to right: Lake Yellowstone Cabins; lobby, Old Faithful Inn; Mammoth Hotel; Old Faithful Snow Lodge

cabins have shower, toilet and sink. Pioneer cabins have a shower, toilet and sink.

Lake Yellowstone Hotel Cabins (late-May to early Oct) are simple duplex units near the Lake Hotel. All have private bathrooms with a shower.

Mammoth Hot Springs Cabins (early May to early Oct) are Frontier motel-style units usually with one or two beds and a shower, sink and toilet. Four hot-tub cabins are available in summer with a queen bed, shower, toilet, sink and a fenced-in 6-person hot tub. Budget cabins are motel-style units with

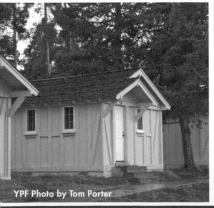

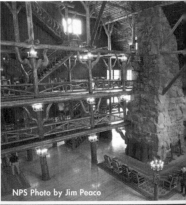

one or two beds and a sink. Shared bathrooms with private showers are nearby.

Old Faithful Lodge Cabins

(mid-May to late-Sept) Frontier cabins are simple motel-style units with a shower, toilet and sink. Budget cabins are basic motel-style units without a bath. Communal showers and bathrooms are located nearby.

Old Faithful Snow Lodge Cabins (early May to late Oct)

all have private baths. Western cabins are motel-style units in modules of 4 with 2 queen beds. Frontier cabins are simple duplex motel-style units with double beds.

Roosevelt Lodge Cabins

(early Jun to early Sept) are Frontier type with 2 double beds, electric heat and a bathroom with shower. Roughrider cabins have wood-burning stoves, typically contain 1 or 2 beds and have no baths. Communal showers and bathrooms are located nearby.

Lodges and Hotels

Canyon Lodge (early Jun to late-Sept) comprises motel-style Dunraven Lodge and Cascade Lodge as well as cabin-style units. Rooms typically have 2 double beds, and private baths. The main lodge provides a gift store, deli, restaurant and cafeteria. Cascade Lodge has 3 floors (no elevators). Dunraven Lodge has an elevator for its 4 floors.

Grant Village (late May to early Oct) motel-style lodgings consist of 6 two-story buildings. All rooms have a telephone and a bathroom with a shower.

Lake Yellowstone Hotel (late-May to early Oct), completed in 1891, is the park's oldest hotel. In 1990 it was restored to its 1920s grandeur. In the Sun Room, guests listen to a string quartet or piano. Lakeside Rooms come with a bathroom and telephone; the number of beds varies per room size. Standard rooms with private bath are located in a two-story building adjacent to the main hotel.

NPS Photo by Jim Peaco

©Gwen Cannon/Michelin

ADDRESSES

Mammoth Hot Springs Hotel (early May to early Oct) was built in 1936 but retains a wing from 1911. In winter, Mammoth has the only park accommodations accessible by wheeled vehicle. Hotel rooms have a telephone, and bathroom with a shower or tub/shower; all have queen beds. Rooms without a bath have a sink and a telephone and usually 2 queen beds. Shared bathrooms with private showers are down the hall.

Old Faithful Inn (mid-May to early Oct) is the world's largest log building. This 6-story National Historic Landmark, designed by Robert Reamer, was constructed in 1903-04. Known as the Old House, the original part of the inn has a huge stone fireplace, whole log columns, and contorted lodgepole pine railings. The East and West Wings were added in 1913 and 1927; many rooms having been remodeled in recent years. Guest rooms come with private or shared baths. A full service restaurant, deli and gift shop are on-site. Decor and amenities vary for rooms in different parts of the inn.

Old Faithful Lodge (mid-May to late-Sept), completed in 1928, is another large log-and-stone-building. This lodge houses a large lobby with great views of Old Faithful Geyser, a cafeteria, bake shop, ice cream counter, gift shop, registration desk and restrooms. There are no guest rooms in the lodge. All lodging is cabin-style (*see p91*).

Old Faithful Snow Lodge (early May to late-Oct) was completed in 1999 of heavy timber construction. It was the first full-service accommodation to open in Yellowstone since the Canyon Lodge in 1911. The interior features wildlife- and park-themed decor. All guest rooms have queen or king beds, full bathrooms and telephones. A full service dining room, quick-service Geyser Grill and Bear Den Gift Shop round out the amenities. In winter, the lodge is accessible by over-snow vehicles only. Reservations for a snow coach can be made by calling 866-GEYSERLAND (866-439-7375). Snow coaches to Old Faithful depart from Mammoth Hot Springs Hotel, West Yellowstone and Flagg Ranch.

Roosevelt Lodge (early Jun to early Sept) opened in 1920, one year after Roosevelt's death, and serves as a rugged hideaway for overnight visitors. The lodge offers guests a broad front porch set out with rocking chairs. The interior boasts massive stone fireplaces in the lobby and a dining room. Handsome wood furnishings and hardwood floors can be seen throughout the common areas. No overnight accommodations are located in the lodge; guests stay the night in 80 rustic cabins surrounding the lodge (*see p91*).

Campgrounds

Yellowstone has 12 campgrounds with more than 2,000 sites, plus backcountry sites. Xanterra Parks & Resorts operates 5 of them, which can be reserved in advance online or by phone. See website below for rules, regulations and opening/closing dates.

Same-day reservations can be made by phone.
The other 7 campgrounds are operated by the National Park Service, and are available on a first-come, first-served basis. Information can be found online at www.nps.gov/yell/planyourvisit.

National Park Service Campgrounds - non-reservations sites			
CAMPGROUND	SITES	FEATURES	RV SITES
Indian Creek	75	V	10 at 40'; 35@30'; pull-through
Lewis Lake	85	V	a few at 25'
Mammoth	85	A, F, G	most are pull-through
Norris	>100	F, G	2 at 50' (signed); 5 at 30'
Pebble Creek	>30	V	some long pull-throughs
Slough Creek	27	V	14 at 30', walk through first to assess sites beyond #16
Tower Fall	31	V	all at 30' or less; has hairpin curve
Xanterra-operated Campgrounds			
Bridge Bay*	>425	A, F, DS, G	call for avail and reservations
Canyon*	272	A,F, S/L, DS, G	call for avail and reservations
Fishing Bridge RV*†	346	F, S/L, G	call for avail and reservations
Grant Village*	425	A, F,S/L, DS, G	call for avail and reservations
Madison*	275	A, F, DS, G	call for avail and reservations
Prices range from about $12 for primitive campgrounds to $20-plus for campgrounds with more facilities. RV sites are higher.			
*Sites you can reserve – Call 866-GEYSERLAND (439-7375) or make online reservations at www.YellowstoneNationalParkLodges.com			
†Sites with and without electricity.			
A Accessible sites available			
F Flush toilets			
V Vault toilets			
S/L Pay showers/laundry onsite			
DS Dump station			
G Generators okay, 8am–8pm			

INDEX

INDEX

Photo credit:
Cover: Grand Prismatic Spring
© Gwen Cannon/MICHELIN
Cover background: Pine trees
© Doug Hudson/Dreamstime.com

Michelin Travel and Lifestyle North America

A division of Michelin North America, Inc.
One Parkway South, Greenville, SC 29615, USA

No part of this publication may be reproduced in any form without the prior permission of the publisher.

© 2012 Michelin North America, Inc.
ISBN 978-1-907099-81-6
Printed: February 2012
Printed and bound in U.S.A.

Moving Forward Means Sustainable Mobility

Moving together towards a world where mobility is more respectful of nature begins with reducing the environmental impact of tires, from their production through the end of their lives. That's why every day, Michelin factories use renewable energy and design tires that can save billions of gallons of fuel globally, and reduce CO_2 emissions. Like you, Michelin is involved in the preservation of our planet.

A better way forward

Coca-Cola®

CELEBRATES

Join us in support of all things beautifu
www.livepositively.com

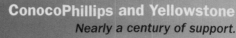

ConocoPhillips and Yellowstone
Nearly a century of support.

In 1872, President Ulysses S. Grant was so moved by Yellowstone's beauty, he declared it a national treasure to be protected and preserved for generations to come. ConocoPhillips has been a proud supporter of Yellowstone National Park for 95 years. Our company has always been committed to protecting the environment while responsibly delivering energy to the world.

And we continue to play our part to secure America's energy future by collaborating with others across a variety of fields to develop new energy sources. By protecting our environment and encouraging sound energy policies, our country can improve environmentally, economically and securely.

ConocoPhillips

There's Power in
Cooperation™

www.conocophillips.com

Yellowstone
National Park

We appreciate everything it is and everything it's not.

Toyota is honored to support Yellowstone National Park and
those who preserve it from red lights, endless blacktop and rush-hour traffic.
May it always remain as nature intended.

Learn Yellowstone.

Since 1933, we've been connecting people to Yellowstone National Park and our natural world through education. We invite you to join the Association and support Yellowstone. While you are here, be sure to:

1. Buy a book, map, or other educational product from one of our nine Park Stores.

2. Take a class or tour with our field school, the Yellowstone Association Institute.

3. Become a member and take advantage of park-wide discounts.

As the park's official nonprofit educational partner, proceeds from our operations support research and education in Yellowstone.

Please stop by any of our Park Stores to join the Association or for more information.

YELLOWSTONE ASSOCIATION

www.YellowstoneAssociation.org

INSPIRE. EDUCATE. PRESERVE.

Working Together For Tomorrow

Canon's corporate philosophy is *"Kyosei"* –
all people, regardless of race, religion or culture,
harmoniously living and working together into the future.
Our Corporate Social Responsibility (CSR) activities are a
reflection of our *Kyosei* philosophy.

*A leading provider of consumer, business-to-business
and industrial digital imaging solutions, Canon takes
pride in being on the frontlines of cutting-edge
technology and innovation.*

NOTES